3, rue Beautreillis
75004 Paris
ISBN 2-906571-26-1

Edited by
JEAN-YVES BOSSEUR

SOUND AND THE VISUAL ARTS

Intersections between Music and Plastic Arts today

with the collaboration of
ALEXANDRE BRONIARSKI

Translated from the French by
BRIAN HOLMES
PETER CARRIER

THIS SERIES EDITED BY DANIELE RIVIERE

IN THE SAME SERIES

IN FAVOUR OF TODAY'S ART, *From the Object of Art to the Art of the Object*
François Dagognet

FOREWORD

The relations between sound, graphic signs and space have tended to grow more and more ambiguous in some spheres of recent artistic production. In this respect, experiments carried out at the beginning of the century by Futurists and Dadaists or, more recently, by John Cage, have figured as invaluable catalysts for artists who have sought to go beyond conventional categories.

In general, attempts to set up an exchange, or even osmosis, between the respective artistic fields, visual and acoustic, have continued up to this day to branch out and become more diversified in nature. In response to this development, we have chosen to examine not the forms of artistic expression which are based on the principles of analogy and metaphor, but rather those which deliberately play on the paradox implied whenever classification becomes an aim in itself, whether at the stage of the conception, or the perception, of these forms. Indeed, numerous composers have drawn inspiration from pictorial works. Even more numerous are the painters who have adopted musical thought, and especially a musical score, as the basis of their reflection, or as a source for immersing their senses prior to pursuing their own particular practice. For most of the time, however, this does not affect the status of their work, or the nature of the artistic support they are using. The influence of another artistic discipline appears as if absorbed into the core of a work which, in fact, retains its original characteristics, either of a score intended for concert performance, or a painting shown in the normal conditions of an exhibition. This does not, of course, undermine the aesthetic validity of such processes.

In the case of other artists, however, the encounter with the problem of accounting for elements which appear extraneous or subsidiary to the practice customarily taught them in art colleges, leads to a profound, and sometimes radical transformation of their artistic output. They begin to see space as an essential dimension of a musical project, and time as a concrete component of any plastic work of art, so that a sound object takes on a double identity in light of both its visual appearance and its acoustic effects. Consequently, we have decided to focus our attention on those phenomena which inevitably bear witness to zones of intersection with others, such as notation, a visualized representation of musical thought, or sound sculpture, 'happenings,' and 'performance' art, not to mention mediums using new technology. These also lead or, ideally, incite the artist to adopt procedures which override academic divisions and favor instead switching from one sphere to the other, which by no means amounts to any unnatural or pretentious attempt at constructing parallel references.

Throughout the course of this enquiry, our encounters with a number of artists may serve as an essential step towards a revival of this debate, and for widening the scope of artistic enquiry, for all of them have in common an approach which puts the essentially elusive nature of the creative act, over and above the traditional opposition between space and time, to the test.

CHAPTER I

The Eye and Musical Notation

The search for a visual representation of musical phenomena and the understanding of space as a full-fledged component of auditive experience can answer extremely divergent aesthetic intentions. This has become clear over the last few decades, as the most deterministic and open-ended tendencies of musical thinking have developed side by side. The visualization of sound through notation permits us, notably, to sound out the status that the composer assigns to the concept of artwork, and the role that he accords to the performer/interpreter.

Observing notation across the successive epochs of written music can help us grasp those characteristics of the sound world that musicians have attempted to privilege, given the mutations of their language. But it would be at the very least imprudent to consider notation, now attaining almost universal acceptance, as the most appropriate tool for codifying musical language. Our "sheet music" corresponds to a conception of writing polarized around the effort to fix certain properties of sound, in particular its pitch and duration. This system shows itself to be highly imprecise, when other aspects such as timbre, mode of attack, intensity, or gesture call for attention. Thus any quest for a notational system applicable to all forms of musical communication risks falling prey to the ambition of imposing a single system of thought and analysis.

In effect, thought and notation influence each other, and the evolution of writing manifestly depends on their interactions and tensions. Moved by the needs of an aesthetic in perpetual evolution, the composer is constantly led to transgress the existing rules of notation; and the implications of the notation to whose emergence he contributes open new avenues for his reflection in their turn. The transformations which occur in his manner of envisaging the inscription of graphic signs on the page cannot help but exercise a powerful influence on his conception of time.

The relative ambiguity of the signs that musicians use to convey their ideas also represents the flexibility of notation, capable of adapting to the most disparate individual and stylistic contexts. Thus notation takes on several functions: it orients the performer's play, furnishes a repertoire from which the composer can draw the conceptual tools of communication, and conserves what will appear as the framework of the piece, a visible manifestation which also allows for analysis and classification. The composer can now call on a whole gamut of infinitely variable models of transmission; it is as though he had to choose, for each compositional project, among diverse "tones of voice," from the most authoritarian to the most tolerant. Still it must be admitted that no notation can claim to assure us total control over a work, or to indicate the exact attitude that the performer should take vis-a-vis that which is fixed by the score.

Composers, of course, have never ceased playing on the score's psychological attraction, its impact on the interpreter; one need only cite the *notations for the eye* imagined in the Renaissance by a musician like Luca Marenzio. Through the role accorded to ornamentation, the Baroque period also offers exceptional testimony to the tension that can reign between graphic space, where the visualization of the ornaments is marked by the highly gestural neumatic notation that issued from the Gregorian chant, and symbolic space, which delimits the architecture of the work.

In the early twentieth century, when certain composers felt the need to expand their inquiries to sounds unexploited by traditional music, the gaps of a notation which had evolved but little over more than a century became evident. It is enough to evoke the scores and projects of Italian futurists like Luigi Russolo, conceived for sound-producing objects whose capacities could not be as precisely controlled as those of musical instruments in the strict sense of the word.

Bartok's comments on the transcription of music based on an oral tradition testify to similar feelings of difficulty. In a letter of 1913 he pointed out: "There are many foreign sounds in the popular melodies, certain *glissandi* of the voice, sounds whose pitch cannot be assessed precisely." To represent such effects, he judged it expedient either to add new signs to the existing body, or to "replace them by a large number of explanations on each page." To indicate pitches smaller than a half tone, for example, composers like Aloïs Haba or Ivan Wyshnegradsky added various sign systems to the previously known symbols.

As experimentation with new sonorous resources widened in scope—notably in the work of Varèse—ramifications of traditional notation revealed themselves to be indispensable. "Since new frequencies and rhythms will have to be indicated for the score, current notation will become inadequate; the new notation will probably be seismographic... As in the Middle Ages, we are confronted with a problem of identity: that of finding graphic symbols to transpose the composer's ideas into sounds." In this way, Varèse gives us a glimpse of a mode of notation "resembling the ideographic writing originally used very early on for the voice, before the development of writing on staves.[1]"

Schoenberg himself made attempts to perfect a system of notation more appropriate to the fundamental mutations he effected in the harmonic domain, a system that would reflect tonal order above all (exactly what was questioned by the founder of dodecaphony). Thus Schoenberg dreamed of a notational system that would accord an equal place to each of the twelve tones of the chromatic scale—exercising in return a determining influence on perception itself.

(1) — Varèse, *Ecrits*, Christian Bourgois, Paris, 1983, p. 93.

The question of notation rapidly overflows that of the vocabulary employed, to concern the problem of fixing both the compositional project—in its most specific dimension—and the results of the interpretation. This is exactly what subtends Schoenberg's remark: "The piece is so orchestrated (or at least, such is my intention) that the sound depends on the performers playing exactly what I have written." But did the state of notation at that time allow him to attain this result?

Although representing a far distant aesthetic, Stravinsky also poses the problem of the imponderables of interpretation, which he attempts to reduce to a minimum when he declares: "I have often said that my music should be *read*, *executed*, but not *interpreted*."

For his part, Honegger foresaw a progressive mechanization of musical givens, to the point where a totally mechanical musical orchestra would replace the one we know. Recent developments in the writing and production techniques of the musical phenomenon have incontestably confirmed his intuitions. But there, of course, it is a question of only one tendency of musical thought, haunted by the idea of an optimal stabilization of the creative project, eliminating all uncertainty with respect to the relation between a particular visual sign and its acoustic consequences.

Other composers more willingly forgo the quest to perenially conserve as many characteristics of a given acoustic organization as possible (after all, the task has been assumed today, and with the greatest fidelity, by the means of mechanical reproduction—leading Bartok to point out that "the only true notations are the grooves of the record itself"). Instead, such composers believe that notation should constitute a catalyst for musical variation. This is why some (Earle Brown, for example) feel much closer—in their work of conceptualization, then of notation and communication—to the tendencies of the Renaissance and the Baroque than to the ideas promoted by Romanticism, which aimed to sacralize the composer's creation by fixing its contours in an immutable way.

In the reconsideration of the norms of notation and the renewal of its visualization, it will therefore be necessary to distinguish between two essentially divergent attitudes: one which contributes to an amplification of the deterministic implications of the preexisting systems, and another which questions the status of the score as object (notably with the advent of the open form). In the first case, the exploration of new dimensions of musical and vocal material has given rise to a considerable growth in the repertory of symbols destined to guide the interpretation. Thus Karlheinz Stockhausen in *Momente* and György Ligeti in *Aventures et Nouvelles Aventures* came to invent an ensemble of signs to suggest actions such as the snapping of fingers, the clapping of hands, cries, or other extra-instrumental interventions. This attempt to perfect a corpus of signs capable of testifying to the diversification of the acoustic elements that can be incorporated into a work is generally accompanied by a will to maximum effectiveness. The player must not be confused by an overabundant delivery of information on the score; like a functional ideogram, the best sign will be the one that accounts for a given sound with optimal clarity and concision. This preoccupation is manifest in Krzystov Penderecki's scores. In a radical split from the pointillistic conception of writing, such as it emerged in post-Webernian serialism, for example, the architectural aspects of pieces like *Tren* or *Anaklasis*—and the notation associated with them—are reduced to only a few vectors, orientations received by human perception with great clarity, in the form of a succession of contrasting sonorous states or a sequence of gradual metamorphoses. Graphic representation takes the lead over the symbolic character of traditional notations: a simple analogical correspondence associates duration with space on the horizontal axis, while the registers of pitch are stacked from low to high on the vertical. These givens, already present in the classical notation system, are exploited here in a much more schematic way; the elements of notation appear "concentrated" to the extreme, to the point where they convey only the most evident traits of the acoustic elements being sought. Eliminating certain constraints of reading, the composer seems to be directing the interpreter's concentration above all toward the production of sound, and not toward signs to be deciphered.

This convergence between the sound phenomenon and the spatial nature of its representation can be found, for example, in G. Ligeti's *Volumina*, an organ score where "clusters" (very tight "bunches" of sound in compact chords) are evoked by black masses of varying thickness, whose slope corresponds to modulations of range. Here we see something like the aspiration to a fusion of the concepts of time and space, through a notation producing an ideal image.

There is no question that the experience of electronics has weighed heavily in this insistence on a visualization of acoustic phenomena, as the existing representational system is yet more inappropriate for compositional intentions linked to electroacoustical operations than for new modes of vocal or instrumental play. In some cases, for example K. Stockhausen's *First Electronic Studies*, the notation invented is precise enough to allow another musician to reconstruct the electronic experimentation from its visual transcription; these cases remain rare, however, as the multiplication of electro-acoustic technologies in the last twenty years has been such that the notation of operations carried out in the studio[2] is far from sufficient for any new realization to actually approach the original on the basis of the "notes" transmitted. It is true, though, that electroacoustic work has contributed to heighten our attention to the minutest details of the sound components in play, which cannot help but render instrumental notation itself more complex and precise. It is naturally quite difficult to evaluate the point at which the accumulation of information can no longer be mastered by the performer. A number of serial scores—for example K. Stockhausen's early *Klavierstücke* or Pierre Boulez's *Premier cahier de structures* (which he had considered entitling *Monument à la frontière du pays fertile*, after a painting by Paul Klee)—practically overflow with cases that push the possibility of reading to its limits. In certain scores,

(2) — For example, K. Stockhausen's most recent electro-acoustic "scores," such as *Telemusik* or *Hymnen*.

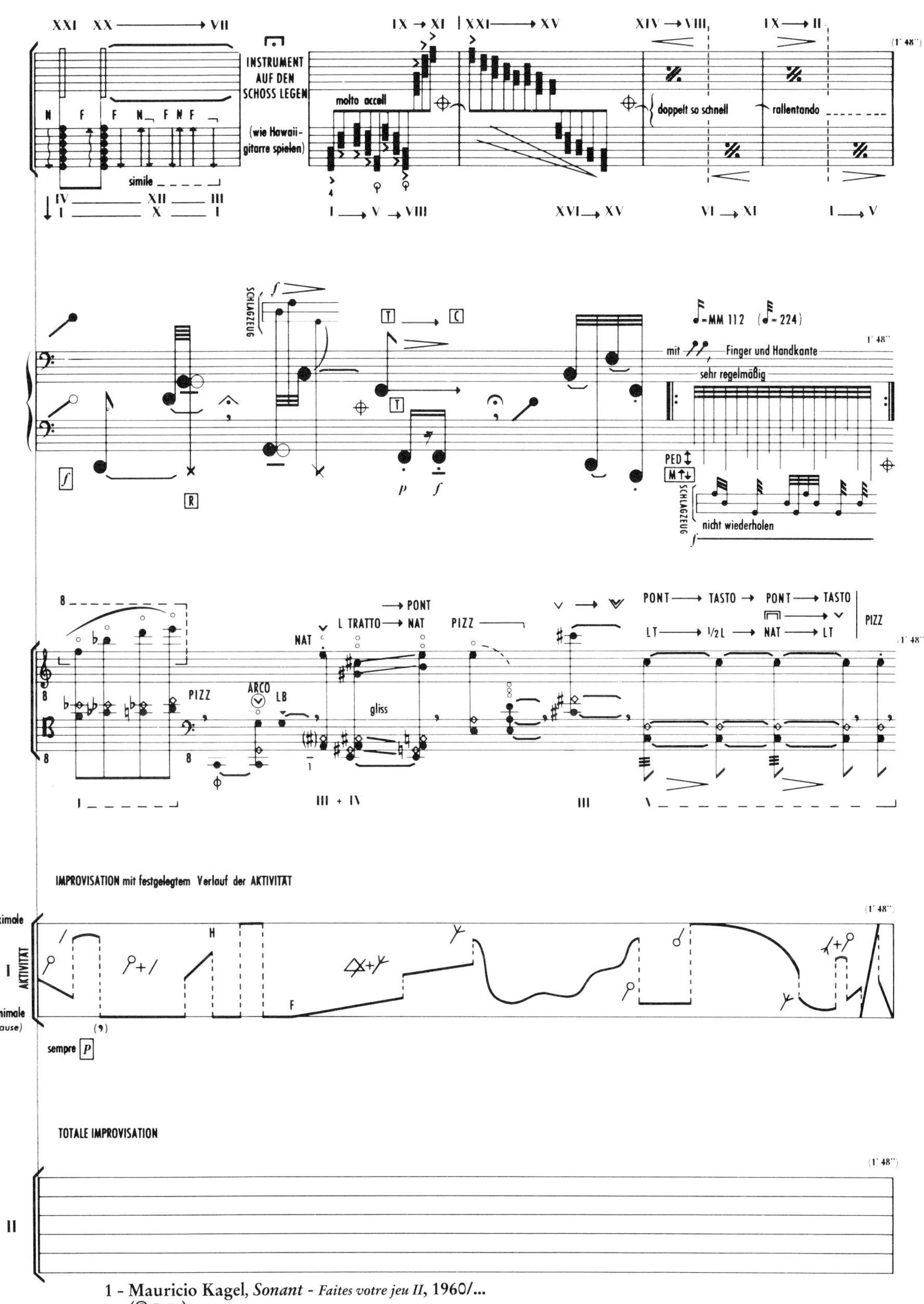

1 - Mauricio Kagel, *Sonant* - *Faites votre jeu II*, 1960/...
(© D.R.)

Mauricio Kagel has gone so far as to "stage" this overabundance of information submitted to the interpreter, such that the latter must clear his own path through the maze of signs.

This deliberate overdetermination of the principles of notation can be found more recently in Brian Ferneyhough's work. Orienting the interpretation toward a transcendence, the musician must suspend his ego along with all personal interpretation, losing himself in the labyrinthic complexity of the indications and striving—as the composer demands in the introduction to the flute piece *Cassandra's Dream Song*—to reproduce the greatest possible number of the details fixed by notation. Thus the score presents itself as a test of force. One may also observe a certain tendency to fetishize the phenomenon of notation in many of the scores written over the last few years, going so far as to make the precision and even the sheer quantity of the annotated details into a veritable criterion of value, both aesthetic and moral: the more meticulous the writing, the more the composer appears able to impose his creative exigencies, and to demand that his function be taken seriously. Assuring oneself an almost total mastery over the musical material—notably with the help of new technologies—has become the ruling idea of a certain official vanguard, and it is clear that the modes of notation perfected to this end already reflect that spirit very well.

Alongside notations which seek to prolong and complete the existing system, others appear more subversive insofar as they aim above all at a rethinking of the relationship between the interpreter and the text written by the composer; it is partially through their intermediary that the composer can attempt to abolish the hierarchy (or strict distinction) between amateur and professional or creator and performer, or even the divisions between artistic disciplines. This is notably the case with the graphic scores of John Cage, Earle Brown, and Christian Wolff. Here, the musician is confronted with a text containing no conventional sign; and though these scores are usually accompanied by verbal instructions which give some indication as to the deciphering of the graphic phenomena elaborated by the composer, the instructions are not conceived so as to provide a univocal response to the questions posed by the notation (if they were, they would merely replace one code by another). By disorienting the musicians, these notations constitute veritable stimuli leading the performers to express themselves through their own sound world, implying that they must play their instrument —alone or in company—without being subordinate to an imposed style, but also without falling back on clichés engendered by habit. In this way, notation becomes experimental in the sense that John Cage gives to the word: what is produced at the time of the realization is not predetermined by the nature of the signs inscribed in the score. Questions rather than orders, incorporated into processes of play rather than object-works, the notations will encounter as many modes of approach as there are individuals: "a question, not an object but rather a process, which finally must be considered as specific to each individual."

December 52 by E. Brown, for example—one of the very first graphic scores—consists of a blank page on which black rectangles of varying widths and lengths are inscribed. Closer observation leads one to remark that two figures of the same dimensions never appear on the page, nor two equal empty spaces. Each figure is therefore individualized and part of a context; each has a specific "weight" of its own. What can one deduce from these with regard to the production of a musical event? The size and placement of the figures can give rise to all sorts of variations in register, intensity, and duration, even if no instrumentation nor any overall playing time is defined. Does the performance then entail an acoustic translation of the impressions received by the eye from the graphics and their disposition on the page? No musical direction seems favored, nor even an order of reading, as there are no staves or points of orientation to lead one way or another. This is why E. Brown speaks of a "composed execution" with regard to *December 52*, and not of an "executed composition"; for the musicians are "implied in the very generation of the work." Brown considers such scores transitional: "The score is an image of this space at an instant which must always be grasped as unreal and transitory... The performer must put it all into motion and enter the image, either staying within it and letting it move, or speeding on through it.[3]"

The forms thus put into play are envisaged as being synergetic, in the sense where synergy implies that the total effect of that which is given by the score—by the "text" in its totality—is greater than the sum of the effects as independently analyzed. It is this dynamic, synergetic effect that renders the process fundamentally open and institutes it as "work in progress." Even more, when E. Brown insists on the definition of synergy as "the conjugated action of all a system's organs," he underlines the fact that, in order to elaborate such processes, one must adopt a different outlook than the one called for by an architectural-type assemblage.

Would graphic representation be the most adequate vehicle to uphold the dynamics of this process, providing it is first cleared of all correspondences and equivalences running more or less parallel to the symbolic representation of sound? "What Pollock created during the last ten years of his existence completely upset my way of conceiving music and made me discover chance forms, which led me to *Available Forms,*[4]" declares E. Brown. For him, "mobile plastic forms cannot in any way constitute models for forms of musical communication, which have their own conditions of existence.[5]" Nonetheless, Brown has declared that he was stimulated in the composition of *Available Forms II* (1961) by the mobiles of Calder, the variability of elements in his own work being comparable to the innumerable relations of form that can emerge from a piece by Calder. "After Pollock, Calder is the one who marked me deeply; his mobiles allowed me to observe free variations taking place, changes that could go on to infinity..."

To deter inclinations toward an understanding of the relationships between graphic presentation and time by means of simplistic and ultimately quite arbitrary deductions, E. Brown insists on the necessity of

(3) — E. Brown, notes for "Folio Pieces," in *An Anthology*, La Monte Young and Jackson MacLow, Heiner Friedrich Verlag, Munich, 1970.
(4) — Interview with Jean-Yves Bosseur, *les Lettres Nouvelles*, October-November, 1966.
(5) — E. Brown, "Sur la forme," in *Musique en Jeu n° 3* , Seuil, Paris, 1971, p. 32.

"extending and intensifying the ambiguity inherent in all graphic representation and in every response that the composer, the performer, and the public can make to it." Ambiguity multiplies the responses, such that each phenomenon—each mode of apprehension—becomes self-sufficient, thrusting aside restrictive intentions that would valorize it only in the light of another event. For those who confront such graphic processes, a difficulty arises from the fact that graphic representation creates an impression of spatial direction to which time risks being subordinated, as though its laws could or should be dictated. In the notes written by Brown in conjunction with the composition of *December 52* and *Four Systems*, the accent falls on the necessity of escaping the directionality of reading so as to attain multiple dimensions of response; the disposition of graphic signs in *December 52*, for example, renders a unidimensional musical reading of the page in accordance with the conventional principles of reading a score rather difficult to conceive.

Intersection III (1953) by Morton Feldman, also commented by J. Cage in the article "Indeterminacy,[6]" constitutes another example of a score whose basic rules give no hint as to the stylistic result foreseen by the composer. The score of this piano piece consists of an assemblage of small boxes corresponding to units of time. On every page are inscribed three bands, each the height of three boxes; these correspond, from top to bottom, to the high, medium, and low registers. The numbers within each box indicate the number of sounds to be produced. The pianist is free to choose any intensity. M. Feldman also stresses that the interpreter is free to introduce the sound or group of sounds at any point within the period of time marked out by the box. The score of *Intersection III* represents a kind of grid: the notation does not suggest the quality of the sound, but rather the possibility that a sound event will occur. As Cage writes in "Composition as Process": "The function of the performer in the case of *Intersection III* is that of a photographer who, on obtaining the camera, uses it to take a picture. The composition permits an infinite number of these,

(6) — J. Cage, "Indeterminacy," in *Silence*, Wesleyan Press, Middletown, 1961.

and, not being mechanically constructed, will not wear out.[7]"

There is no drive, in J. Cage's music, to achieve coherency between the compositional structure, the notation, and the resultant sound; composing, noting, playing, and hearing can be considered autonomous actions which do not have to be linked by relations of cause and effect. This encourages the shattering of the work: it is no longer an object closed in on itself, but a dynamic organism which the interpreter is to bring to life, and not only to completion. Cage has employed methods of chance in his compositional work, a highly cultivated method in the case of the *I Ching* (used, for example, in *Music of Changes*, 1951), as well as more anarchic methods, like casting dice or observing the imperfections in paper (*Concert for piano*, 1957-1958) or an astronomical atlas (*Atlas Eclipticalis*). With the *Variations* and *Cartridge Music*, however, he pushes aside all reference to traditional musical writing and leaves the interpreter the task of defining the musical material to be associated with the process proposed. Yet this should not be understood as a transmission or substitution of power; the composer does not throw back on the performer the authority that he had previously assumed, but tends rather to share the potential indetermination contained in what is more a "process" of play than a score in the traditional sense of the term. In *Variations*, *Cartridge Music*, or *Theater Piece*, Cage invites individuals who can no longer define themselves exclusively as musicians, actors, or dancers, to take part in a game, letting sounds be produced in the most objective manner possible, and therefore letting time flow by without trying to impose an absolute measure. With the exception of *Variations V*, which brings a lighting system, a group of dancers, and an electroacoustic device into play, *Variations I to VI* can be realized with any sound-making resources. The different scores are essentially composed of transparent plastic sheets on which are inscribed points, circles, and lines; each of the *Variations* is accompanied by instructions for the disposition and deciphering of the resultant graphic figures.

(7) — J. Cage, "Composition as process," in *Silence*, Wesleyan Press, Middletown, 1961.

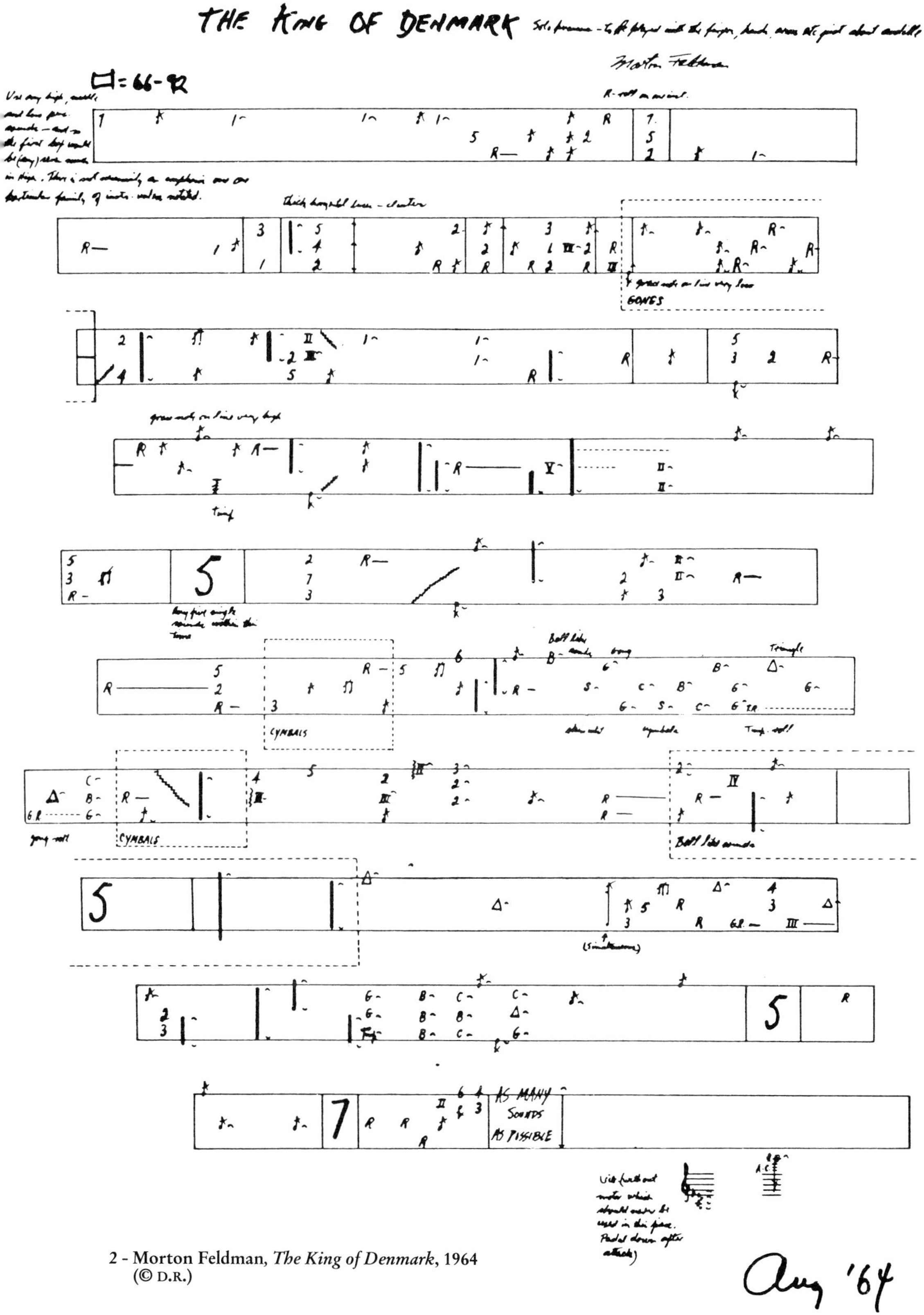

THE KING OF DENMARK

Morton Feldman

□ = 66-92

GONGS

CYMBALS

CYMBALS

AS MANY SOUNDS AS POSSIBLE

Aug '64

2 - Morton Feldman, *The King of Denmark*, 1964
(© D.R.)

In the same spirit, *Cartridge Music* (1960) comprises twenty sheets —on which are reproduced from one to twenty forms—and three transparent sheets, one sprinkled with points, the other with small circles, the third traversed by a dotted line; a fourth transparent sheet, representing the face of a clock, is laid atop the others to help define (in a non-mechanical but rather "craftsman-like" fashion) the duration of the events to be produced. The combinations, superimpositions, and intersections of the different figures invite one or several musicians to set a program of actions. The overall time of execution and the nature of the sound-material are free: only the amplification of "small sounds" and the use of an electric piano or a cymbal are counseled. The formal schemas of *Cartridge Music* can be applied to any sound source—indeed, to any mode of activity—and also to the organization of existing compositions. Cage has even used them to define the form of some of his lectures.

In J. Cage's work, the act of notation does not close upon the constitution of an object; it is given to be grasped in the moment, as a catalyst whose impact is not to be sought in possible consequences, but perhaps in the contemporaneousness of a singular appearance.

Some people consider such experiments—where the concept of the work is reduced to its simplest expression—as a form of abdication on the composer's part. On the contrary, one can see such processes as enlarging the possibilities of a form, transforming the work into a pure potential, "a field of infinitely extensible forces."

The diverging modalities of the experience of sound in writing, playing, and hearing, and the recognition of the musical event as a theater of sound-actions, have provoked composers like Mauricio Kagel and Dieter Schnebel to reconsider musical supports. For them, the score—which had formerly been a mere intermediary destined to fade away behind the musical phenomenon par excellence, the performance in concert—can become an active element of this theater, with the most unexpected ludic capacities. This is what takes place, for example, in pieces like M. Kagel's *Prima vista* or *Diaphonie*, where the score is communicated to the musicians in the form of projected slides, bringing about a kind of complicity with the members of the audience, who discover the slides along with the musicians.

One can, however, spot a certain tendency toward mannerism in this visual perspective on notation, or this "artistic graphism." There is, no doubt, something fundamentally baroque in the profusion of graphic elements used by Sylvano Bussotti, which seem to add an aura of sublimity to the musical signs, in a score proposed as an object of contemplation. Distanced from their primary function, conventional notations become so many pretexts for interpretive extrapolations, which are at least partially dependent on the musician's imagination.

By according an overly marked priority to questions of notation, by amplifying the visual characteristics and the formal dimension of the signs—as in the scores of Anestis Logothetis or Roman Haubenstock-Romati—one runs the risk of making them an end in themselves, of letting these graphic preoccupations serve as a substitute for problems of composition, and thus diverting musical activity from its fundamental relationship with the public. These were the considerations that motivated Cornelius Cardew to draft a self-critical assessment of his graphic score *Treatise* in his book *Stockhausen Serves Imperialism*. For him, this is a characteristic trait of the vanguard attitude that he himself pursued for many years: twist reality at will, pose it as a game, slap one logic atop another, operate by diversion and falsification.

The late sixties saw the development of another kind of score, one which owed a great deal to the rise of collective creation: the "verbal score." In this case the score, written with words, becomes a scenario that the musicians memorize and take as the basis for their actions and reactions during the moment of play. This recourse to a text-score has shown itself to be an entirely new way of envisaging the transmission of a musical concept, provoking among the performers an original and less formalized—because less encoded—type of communication, one that calls more on the personality of each individual than traditional notation did, because it is less preoccupied with the point-by-point reproduction of every detail of the composition. Verbal scores—as conceived by Karlheinz Stockhausen, Christian Wolff, Luc Ferrari, Costin Miereanu, Vinko Globokar— simply constitute so many different incitements to produce a musical action, generally in a group; the composer becomes the catalyst of an action whose basic conditions are, of course, still exposed by him, but where the score disappears as a material object interposed between a musician and his partners, allowing musical ideas to evolve in an open-ended way.

Clearly, the establishement of new signs (or modes of approach) with regard to musical play was not necessarily dictated by a strictly didactic intent. It is evident, on the other hand, that numerous scores which leave a large measure of initiative to the performers— through the employ of graphic forms or verbal suggestions—represent a form of apprenticeship, a way of listening, which ought to be more widely taken into account today. Some musicians, musicologists, and publishers seem to have too rapidly relegated these experimental notations and open forms to the panoply of sixties' accessories. After the effects of fashion and their excesses have passed, much remains to be discovered in scores and notational principles that permit the overcoming of divides between different types and levels of musical education, and thus encourage all sorts of currents of exchange. For this, however, the channels of information must keep up with the plurality of movements in current thinking—which is far from being the case in the small, institutionalized ghetto of so-called avant-garde music.

If the extension of the musical vocabulary on one hand, and the evolution in the composer's attitude to the performer on the other, have provoked the definition of new systems of symbolic and graphic signs to account for the aesthetic conceptions of instrumental and vocal play, the shattering of form by mobile works has also contributed to transform the physical aspect of the score. Since the early variable-form works—such as K. Stockhausen's *Klavierstück XI* (1956) or the *Troisième sonate pour piano* (1957) by Pierre Boulez (printed in two colors for a better visualization of its formal components), followed by André Boucourechliev's *Archipels* and certain scores by Francis Miroglio—the relation of the notations to their spatial context has undergone significant changes. Thus *Klavierstück XI* is reproduced on a 53 x 93 cm sheet containing nineteen irregularly spaced sequences, no longer calling for a linear, right-to-left reading. The pianist must bring his perception of the space of the page into play, like the reader of Mallarmé's *Coup de dés* or certain poems by Apollinaire.

Just as the variability of the form provoked the fabrication of books whose mode of presentation adheres to the process involved (c.f. Raymond Queneau's *Mille milliards de poèmes*), similarly the score, given its potentially mobile operations, can become a kind of book-object calling for certain types of manipulation. Thus, in order to realize a version of Henri Pousseur's *Miroirs de votre Faust*, the pianist must engage in a process of "scooping out," creating something like windows in the score. Depending on the way the sheets are folded and on the types of windows created, the musical content and the articulation of its different parts can vary greatly.

The relationships with the plastic arts are a theme of predilection for F. Miroglio, as attested by *Ping Squash* (1979), a percussion piece written in homage to A. Calder who, in 1930, had elaborated a "sound mobile," the only one he ever constructed: *A White Ball, a Black Ball.* F. Miroglio retains this mobile's "functional principle," but "diversifies its possibilities for timbre so as to integrate it into the sonorous continuum of the composition."

A Calder mobile had also been used as a "conductor" by E. Brown in his *Calder Piece* (1963). The four percussionists were to change their modes of attack as well as other characteristics of play according to the proximity or distance of the mobile's elements to each one of them.

This proliferation of new signs and notational principles has not, of course, gone unremarked by a certain number of painters; it has occasionally even given rise to collaborations. Thus, after having realized a first graphic score-book, *Opus incertain* (1981), the painter Félix Rozen undertook research using the means provided by the UPIC (Polyagogic Composition and Information Unit), a machine invented by Iannis Xenakis in the framework of the CEMAMU (Center for the Study of Musical Mathematics and Automatics). In effect, this machine allows for the association of graphic forms and acoustic results through a graphic screen linked to a micro-computer and its terminals. More recently, F. Rozen (working with Marc Battier at the IRCAM in Paris) has elaborated a piece for magnetic tape, entitled *Spectral* (1984). If one may speak of an effective osmosis of the sonorous and the visual in this approach, it is because the process of learning of musical structures has been able to "inform" F. Rozen's plastic experience. In return, what he has learned through painting about expression, sensuality, and materials has influenced his musical work. From his perspective, his current inquiries in the domain of music flow naturally from his pictorial activity, the latter having become a veritable systematization of visual expression through the serial repetition of motifs which seem to have neither beginning nor end.

For Christian Rosset, who realized a certain number of graphic scores in the seventies—before turning the greater part of his musical activity to the definition of new forms of radiophonic music—there is also no break between activity as a plastic artist and as a composer: both imply a physical rapport to writing, instigating a compositional procedure which is more bodily than strictly conceptual.

The vocabulary of sound is now limitless, to our greater benefit today; can it then accomodate a system of writing to be shared by all, a standardized "sheet music"? Can the variability of implications springing from the sound phenomenon—a variability we can actively live, as soon as we decide to cast aside the restrictive dogma and the prohibitions of schooled music—be matched by anything other than a plurality of models of transmission? Should we then regret the fractured aspect of current notation, and condemn the fact that, for many

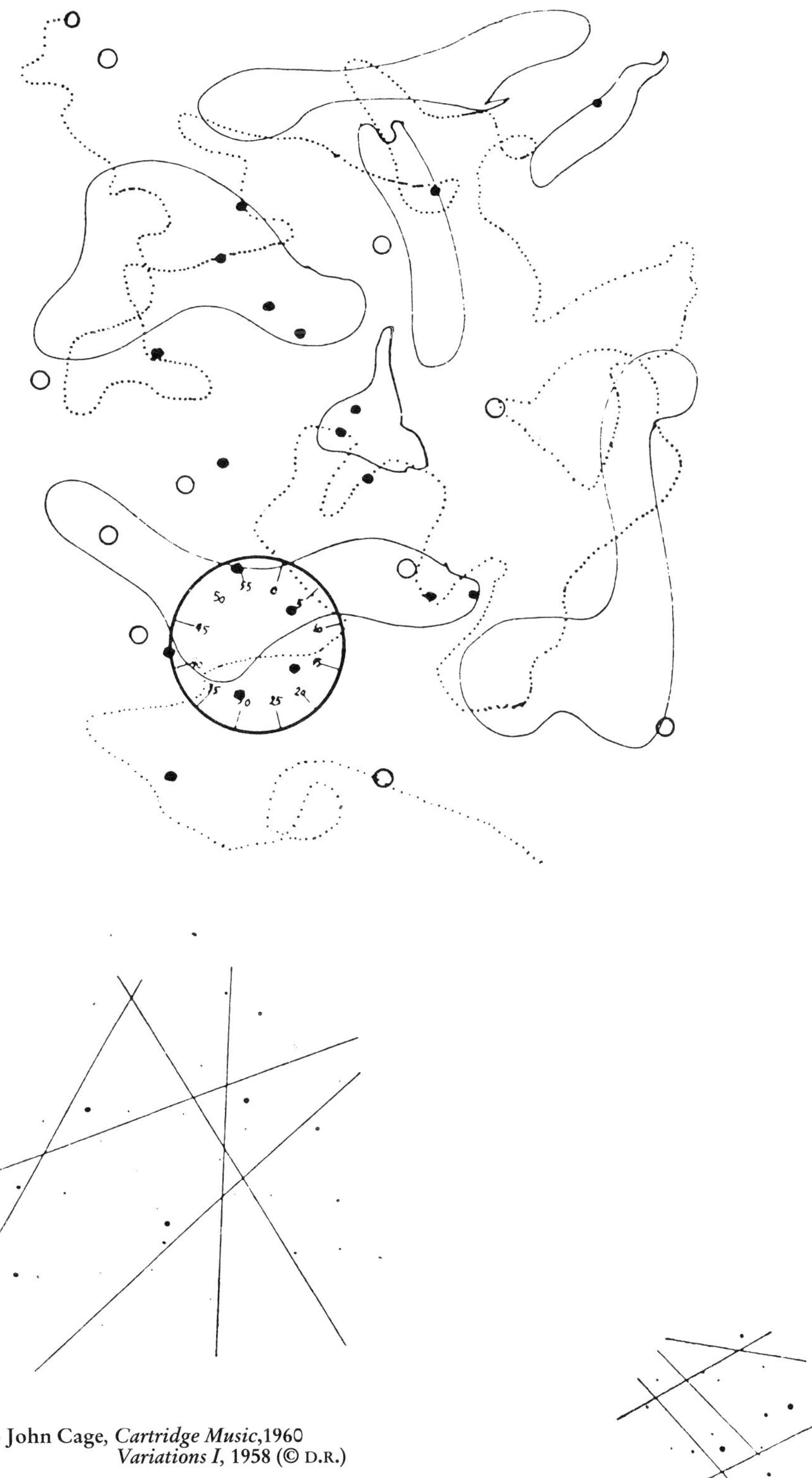

3 - **John Cage**, *Cartridge Music*,1960
Variations I, 1958 (© D.R.)

composers, there exist as many approaches to notation as there are works? In the diversity of their physiognomies, the scores written over these past three decades show the degree to which the choice of a notation belongs directly to the process of creation. They also show that the musician's debate does not simply revolve around the distance to be taken from the norms of traditional notation: it is a question of rethinking, for each score, the level of information and the mode of communication to be brought into play, as a function of the specific properties of each project.

Francis Miroglio

One can imagine that the visual aspect of all musical notation already provides a particularly stimulating range of interactions. Has the advent of graphic notation been a decisive factor for you?

My involvement in this field began following my encounter, around 1965, with Alexander Calder, and it is worth noting in this respect that we have made two ballets together.[8] His research in the field of plastic arts has been very important for me. What's more, it's thanks to him that I got involved with the Maeght Foundation and subsequently found myself within the circle of painters who were evolving within this privileged framework. As a result, I literally plunged headfirst into visual creation. Of course, a certain form of osmosis occurred and, over the years, my music rather swiftly turned towards certain forms of notation which granted a place for what one might call the notion of "mobility" in music (a question which had actually concerned me well before I met Calder). From this moment on, we were intent on rendering this notion of mobility tangible and apprehensible for musicians, and were, therefore, more or less forced to keep within the norm as far as graphics were con-

(8) — *Eppursimuove* (1965), *Notre Monde* (1966), *Espaces 3* (1967)

cerned. It was also more worthwhile to use an efficient form of pictography rather than written explanations, for although the latter are possibly, but by no means certainly, more precise, the former prove to be internationally more recognizable.

And in this respect, certain plastic artists have played an important role...

During 1966-67, I also met Miró, with whom I produced *Projections* in 1968. Joan Miró did a selection of gouaches to contribute towards the making of this work and, in particular, for the title page of the score. *Projections* is a string quartet which is played along with fifty-eight photographic slides, some of which are of original plates. In more precise terms, the word "projections" has several levels of meaning. In fact, the very multiplicity of the word "projection" interested me a lot, which is why most of the titles of my works are in the plural form. On the one hand, by taking this word at its face value, it means the projection of images which are representative of Miró's work and, for me in particular, it means the projection of visual images onto auditory sound, a certain type of superimposition or, more exactly, conjunction between these different artistic disciplines. At the same time, it also refers to the action of projecting or, in other words, releasing the sound proposals created by the various musicians of the string quartet, together with the mobile responses which they can choose according to the proposals on offer to them. A dialectical relation is then established between the visual and auditory aspects in so far as the musicians of the string quartet take part, in their own way, in the visual aspect of the piece, their visual impact on the slides consisting in them standing up from time to time to play their solo parts, whereby their silhouettes are projected onto the screen showing the slides. It's a form of trilogy—sonorous, visual and plastic—all of which operates simultaneously as a whole.

Did the original gouaches made by Miró for Projections *have any relation to your own musical vocabulary, or did he work on the basis of certain elements which you had suggested to him musically?*

His gouaches essentially form the basis for the titles of the various parts of the score. This work was done in two phases. One of these involved long discussions beween the two of us to select the slides (originating from different periods of time). Miró also gave his opinion about the subtitles and the various sections of the score. To my mind, it is also extremely important that the essence of visual and musical relations should be concentrated on differences or similarities of density, because I think this notion of density is one of the most important areas of common ground on which the visual and the auditory may meet. In fact, density represents an arithmetic parameter which can be defined as the number of visual or auditory events produced within a given space or time, the latter serving as a reference point by which density can be measured. For sound, this can be one second. For visual elements, the reference could be, for example, one cubic centimeter. The system of reference is variable, but must be defined in relation to the proportions of the subject under consideration. Henceforth, stable, variable, strong or weak densities, whether in the process of increasing or decreasing, can be defined in comparison.

Have you had any other opportunities to bring together slides and live instrumental playing?

Yes, in *Trip Through Trinity*, a work for solo percussion structured around the number 3, a mathematical element operating at every level. It applies, for example, to the number of instruments set to resonate, since there are 33 percussion instruments. One can count a total of 333 different structures, and the length of the score can last 3333 seconds, which goes to show that the whole piece is precisely structured. As far as the visual aspect is concerned, I have associated this music with the screen projection of slides of contemporary paintings, ranging from Kandinsky, Klee, Braque and Picasso, to Bury, Tapiès and a few young painters. All these works have one common denominator, which is to represent triangles. Here again, the number 3 is paramount, whether at an immediately apprehensible visual level, or a little more concealed (less perceptible at first sight). The same goes for the density, as this aspect seems important to me. In this score, there are also what I wouldn't exactly say are similarities, because fortunately similarities cannot exist, but rather parallels between the sounds obtained with percussion instruments and the visual impressions arising from specific paintings.

Your score Ping Squash *is related to Calder's work...*

In actual fact, *Ping Squash* was written after Calder's death as a homage. Calder was a great friend for me. He played a decisive role for the history of contemporary art, and I think his research on mobility influenced all the experiments in kinetic art. I'm quite sure it's a homage because, in the 1930s, he devised a unique sound mobile, the principles of which I adapted in part—without forgetting to mention that the original was Calder's invention—by amplifying its acoustic efficiency, for the original gave out only a limited range of noises and sounds. *Ping Squash* is a sort of sonorous match between two percussionists who play their instruments with table tennis bats, producing unusual sonorities. This is then interrupted by a parameter of mobility operating both at the level of the percussionists' playing, and at the level of the sounds obtained by the movements of the two mobiles, these adopting a perfectly aleatory method for giving indications to the interpreters. A third percussionist also takes part in the proceedings by arbitrating between the other two. His role is to eliminate improvisation—for there are, after all, very rigorous rules and norms in this match—by supplying timbres and by interposing sound elements which can be considered as aleatory, but which occur at precise moments during the course of the playing.

When you used counterpoints of slides in relation to your works, what were you looking for exactly? We have already established the fact that similarities could be dangerous, so is it now more relevant to be talking of structural conformity?

I have never planned a score in relation to a single painting, for these are musical works which can function in conjunction with several paintings. Even when they are all by the same artist, as is the case with

Miró, the artist didn't restrict himself to works corresponding to only one structural form. The mobility of structures and the variety of possible choices form decisive elements in the playing. For me, mobility has always been an essential aspect in music, because I think that today's artists are surrounded by multiple forms of mobility. It seems essential, if not entirely natural and normal, that this mobility should be perceptible in the music I write. In fact, it's by extending this notion to the parameter of timbre that, as early as 1960, I opened up the way for superimposing different instrumentations. Many of my scores are actually playable with several different instrumental formations, each open to being superimposed on the other.

Are there any dimensions of the relation between music and the plastic arts which you find are leading towards a sort of dead end?

It is obvious that everything which arises solely from a musician's impression of plastic works of art is, to my mind, infinitely too subjective to be put to use as a link between music and the visual arts. There has been an enormous quantity of attempts to do this, and they had no value except for single individuals—a factor which for me, when all is said and done, renders them void of interest. To be precise, what interested me is the possibility to work on structural relations in conjunction with pictorial works. I regret the fact that young musicians today take too little interest in painting, and I believe that they have a lot to learn about structure and form, from the plastic artists of their own generation, for example. The composers willing to commit themselves to this research remain few and far between.

Who do you have in mind?

André Boucourechliev has taken an interest in this notion of mobility, that's for sure. Earle Brown as well. But I insist on getting things straight: Earle Brown composed a work called *Calder Piece* where one of Calder's mobiles is employed by being set in rotation by the four percussionists. The mobile plays the role of the conductor. This is saying a lot, because the action of the mobile involves turning on its own axis, and it obviously doesn't turn in a thousand and one dif-

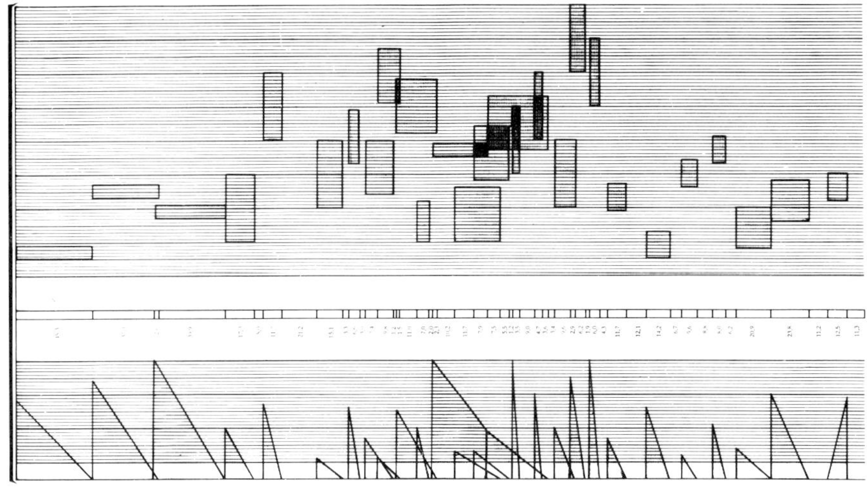

4 - Karlheinz Stockhausen, *Elektronische Studie II*, 1954
(© Universal Editions)

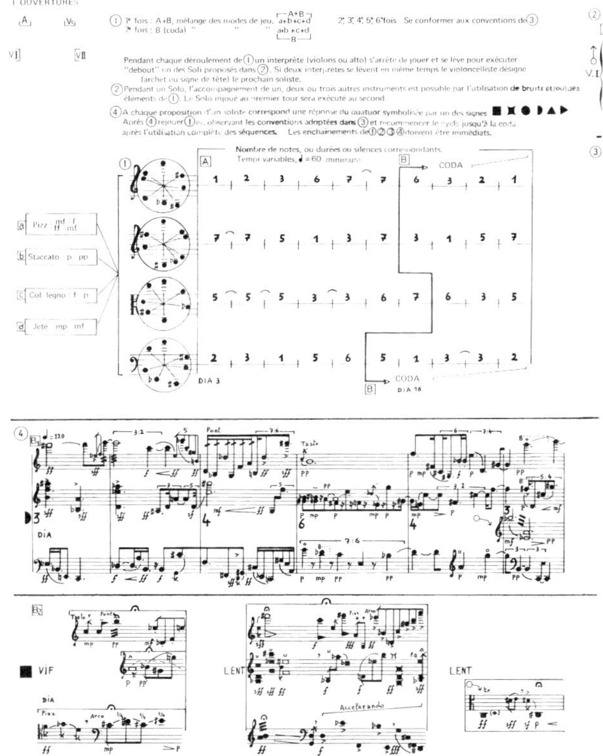

5 - Francis Miroglio, *Projections*, 1967 (fragment)
(© Universal Editions)

ferent ways if you consider that the mobile, chosen and lent by Calder, was not even remotely intended to be put to such use. In other words, the percussionists limit themselves to striking or scraping certain blades of the mobile, which has no tonal quality whatsoever. Besides, Earle Brown ended up by realizing this himself, because he subsequently composed a second version, adding lots of extra percussion instruments which don't take into consideration the sonority of the mobile.

Have you composed other scores in connection with a plastic artist?

Réfractions for four instruments (flute, violin, piano and percussion). This score was composed in reaction, or rather "refraction," against the *Assemblage* of six painting-drawings by Michel Seuphor. It's a score which somehow reproduces the horizontal, vertical and oblique lines of the assemblages created by Michel Seuphor, albeit by reversing these lines. What we have here is a reaction to intersecting lines and plastic structures. The title *Réfractions* was chosen because the parts drawn in white in Seuphor's drawings are found in black in the scores, and vice versa in certain cases. This score consists of six sequences, with a mobile form, causing both a visual and auditory effect on the listener, who is a spectator at the same time. I must stress that if these works, as a whole, succeed in combining plastic arts and music, it is because I have always found it most important to underline the visual aspect contained in music, and even the element of show, as a show to be seen. In music, there are as many things to be seen as there are to be heard. To my mind, this by no means detracts from the music or from the attention it merits from listeners. Percussion, to take one example of a group of instruments, is a real show in itself. A big orchestra is also a show. Seeing an instrumentalist playing, a virtuoso or even a musician in an orchestra or a string quartet, provides an aesthetic touch, an element of beauty and interest which I find decisive.

When you worked with these structural intersections between visual and acoustic spheres, were there any resistances, any paradoxes or difficulties to overcome, which one might expect in view of the specificity of these two types of thought?

Yes. There is a danger of degenerating into the realm of anecdotes, although this can easily be controlled, depending on the type of thought one works in. The more immediate risk is that of imposing a spontaneous, rather superficial reaction to the visual work, onto the musical composition.

Does this therefore entail analyzing both types of phenomenon?

Yes, naturally.

But is it possible to be led to find contradictions just because each kind of analysis doesn't necessarily fit in with the other? Even if you are fully aware of the pitfalls in this work, isn't there always a risk of heading towards a dead end when you consider that each way of thinking is so different?

I quite understand your argument, but I think there are different ways of responding when faced with "seen" structures in relation to music. This can be established according to obvious conformities or parallels between the two, and similarly with respect to contradictions. The latter case is just as revealing, because by opposing phenomena one brings out the qualities of each in relation to the other.

This means, therefore, that when you confronted manners of musical and plastic play in the same space, and at the same time, you were also playing on their relative autonomy?

Exactly.

So you consider that each field has its own mode of being...

Yes. The main criticism of *Projections* was that it didn't take account of the element of color contained in Miró's work. However, and this is one of the more interesting factors, it's not by chance that I chose a string quartet, which provides a relatively common tonal and visual colour. Within the make-up of the string quartet, there occur very specific and original ways of playing—or at least there did at that time, between 1966 and 1967—which effectively introduced a diversity of color. In addition, the unity of timbre produced by the strings enhances the variety of Miró's coloration. In other words, there is a whole give and take—dare I say a dialectic—between these different elements.

Have you never been tempted to establish exact connections between a given color and a given timbre?

No, because for me, this is a purely subjective element. A spectator-listener who hears and sees such a connection might well have a completely different impression of the piece than someone else.

When you organize your graphics for notation, do you then have the impression that you are acting as a plastic artist?

That's not what I have in mind, because one cannot forget that musical writing, even when it is graphic, is intended for interpreters whose task is to give it expression through their playing. Therefore, what I aim for above all is efficiency and a maximum of precision. This is how I have been led to develop not the musical theory of a new type of notation, but, instead, a graphic notation which remains clearly logical. I don't see why, when all string instrumentalists today know how to produce a 'Bartok pizz', and know how it is notated, anyone could be inclined to write it down in any other way, because the acoustic result obtained is just the same whether traditional, or new graphic notation is used. This is why I adhere to what might be called the classical tradition of writing pitch by adding other signs which enable me to obtain a variety of pitches, in particular quarter or third tones, and even networks of pitch.

Some composers have tried to substitute one code for another, others have tried to put the interpreter in an ambiguous situation and to take advantage of his or her disorientation. What is your attitude towards this procedure?

I don't think that the composer should, in some way or another, relinquish his responsibility. If the interpreters are sufficiently talented and imaginative to improvise, they will be capable of coping with anything, regardless of the circumstances, without the composer having to give them the slightest indications. In that case, I can understand quite well why it may be useful to try out a graphic symbol, which from that moment on becomes a pictorial gesture, one which subsequently influences an interpreter who transforms it into a musical gesture. However, I find that all this conceals a grave danger, for it assumes in advance that the instrumentalist is equipped with original imaginative faculties. A limited number of performers do live up to this criterion, but they are by no means bound to do so. Another answer to your question would be that interpreters who are not possessed of such talents will simply take no interest in this sort of music.

Although you may not work with notation as a graphic stimulus for the imagination of the musician, the mobile forms do, however, necessarily interact with space, within the score itself...

That can't be avoided.

Then you too must be in the position of a graphic artist...

Yes, that's true. I can't deny that, of course.

Do you work on this aspect consciously?

Yes, without a doubt.

Always aiming for effectiveness above all, or sometimes also looking to create a score-object?

This is not an insignificant aspect of my approach. Much of the score for *Projections* can actually be regarded as a graphic object.

And you actually envisaged the score as a graphic object as you wrote it?

Absolutely. But I knew at the same time that it corresponded to a style of graphics defined by Miró which would be projected at the same time. What's more, I forgot to mention that four out of the fifty-eight slides designed to accompany this score show representations of the score itself. The reason for this is that there are noticeable graphic similarities between what is written, what one sees, and what one hears.

All of which creates an echo-like effect in respect to what one can hear.

A double echo.

One question which crops up very often relates to the perception of this mobility, whereby it becomes obvious that a plastic mobile, whose functions are immediately apparent to the eye, cannot be compared with a musical mobile. Do you therefore take care to enable the listener to be aware that the piece is destined to move at the instant you determine the musical material proper?

This clearly raises the major question of mobility on the acoustic level, because the listener only ever hears one version, which is by nature a fixed version, as it's the only one on offer. However, I think that sometime in the future it will be possible to make recordings which will allow the listener to compare two mobile versions of the same piece. For example, my piece for six percussion instruments, *Extensions 2*, presents two different versions of the same score on the same record. What also comes to mind is a piece like *Réseaux* for solo harp, that can be played according to different versions, these also lending themselves to superimposition (harp solo, harp and string quartet, harp and orchestra). It might be possible to conceive of a record with concentric grooves permitting the needle to switch from one version to another via special "grade crossings," since the part for harp never changes. With the videodisc of tomorrow, one might well be able to envisage "shunting" the score like trains, from one track to another. Computer technology is already capable of transcribing music and, to cite another sort of evolution, it's worth pointing out that, in 1985, I produced the first score on Minitel. *Mosaïques* is graphic music for seven instruments symbolized by diagrammatical drawings. Written with the help of pictograms based on squares, this piece can be consulted on Télétel, the French electronic telephone directory.

(Paris, March 19, 1992)

Tom Phillips

The work of Tom Phillips defies all restrictive notions of style and all bids to establish fixed aesthetic categories. The multiple, though by no means overdiversified, ways in which Phillips approaches plastic phenomena seems to stem from his exceptional capacity for getting involved in every field which is liable to become a key reference for a work or a series of works (e.g. a "livre trouvé" like *A Human Document* by W. H. Mallock, the backbone of his work over a number of years; a Dogon statuette; the *Divine Comedy* by Dante...).

The experience of time seems to play a fundamental role in the work of Tom Phillips. In view of its constituant elements, each piece implies a certain sort of "maturing" process during the performance time, in particular when works appear in the form of series of variations, which take the shape of several successive "movements." It has often been shown, more or less explicitly, how both memory and time can cut across every pictorial proof. This being the case, at the crossroads of various modes of communication, his approach becomes fundamentally ambiguous. If what Tom Phillips produces partially escapes the category of plastic arts and is occasionally presented as "poetry written by a non-poet" or "composition by a non-composer," as he himself declares with reference to *A Humument*, it is not because he seeks to emulate the ambition of total art, but because the necessity which sparked off his artistic project was itself generated by his preoccupation with the intersecting of space and duration. In this respect, every vaguely dualistic position was doomed to fail to take account of real life situations in all the complexity of their separate parts. This is how, towards the middle of the 1960s, he was led to putting to paper the idea for several graphic scores, in which plastic and musical stimuli succeed in blending into a single project. Scores like these enable us to take stock of the problem of notation and graphically written forms on the basis of a dual perspective which very few composers or painters have previously had the chance of apprehending.

The musical output of Tom Phillips is much more than a side aspect of his activity as a painter, in that it lends an original dimension, along experimental lines, to the relation between musician and score.

"All the pieces I have written are various examples of phenomena in the process of becoming music, phenomena which are rooted in my consciousness and emerge in the form of music, for this was the one and only thing I was able to do with them. [...] While I was compiling the book *A Humument*, there were fragments of text left aside and, seeing as I dislike wastage, I wanted to put these fragments to some other use. They awoke in me all sorts of musical directions, including suggestions for scenery, movements on stage, sonorous events... Finally, I made an assemblage of all the various suggestions which came to mind, and found that they combined to form a huge plan for an opera, that these chunks of text were slowly taking shape as the opera *Irma*."

The aesthetic tendencies of composers like John Cage, Earle Brown, Christian Wolff, and Cornelius Cardew have, to a great extent, worked their way into his scores, which consequently appear to the listener to be just as much an evolving process of playing as a rounded-off work of art.

"If we were to speak of everything which becomes music, the first thing to be pointed out would be that every phenomenon can become music so long as it comes up against the mind of someone who, either by nature or professionally, is a composer. There is no contradiction between the activities of music and of plastic arts, because they originate from one and the same source, the only difference being that I may be more gifted in one than in the other. [...] The majority of ideas which seemed to be the most interesting in the 50s and 60s were common to both painters and musicians... An artist like John Cage was in the forefront of this school of ideas, and he brought them to life perhaps even more radically than the painters—this is why collaborating with composers was an extremely important stimulus for me at all times."

Tom Phillips makes light work of writings in the form of symbolic, graphic, or verbal notations. Just as he maintains a great variety of relations with the field of music, ranging from collage-portraits of composers, via standard scores, to conceptual musical projects (presented in the form of postcards, for example), the consequences of these works depends very much on the way in which the spectator-listener lends an ear or an eye to understand them. A process in which Tom Phillips regards seeing, reading or playing as becoming a choice, or responsibility, which each individual should take on according to his or her capacities. Such projects are in fact indispensable catalysts for the imagination, open forms begging to be deciphered, assimilated and carried on into the future according to everyone's desire to play.

"I am a composer in the same way as a pianist without hands could be a pianist. This is something I never stop thinking about, but which I can't really handle in its entirety because I lack a whole range of technical expertise. Nevertheless, an idea for a composition allows me to get ahead with all sorts of pieces of work. Some of these are in fact linked to the feeling I have for music and actually emerge as unplayable pieces, ones based on the almighty five lines of the stave, which dominate the life of a musician from cradle to grave. These five lines are of cardinal importance for him, and for me too, because I read a lot of scores and, in one way or another, this frequently surfaces very intensely in my paintings. Other phenomena whose distant connections appear to have very little to do with music, at least at first sight, sometimes possess invaluable musical impulses when they are produced rhythmically or dynamically."

Whenever Tom Phillips makes artistic use of a notation or a musical instrument, he insinuates an interpretation of both temporal and spatial character, unveils possibilities for reading and interpreting these works equally well on the basis of their sonorous or plastic merits, as if he intends to trigger off chain reactions. Tom Phillips draws on his diverse experience in the field of music, as a listener, instrumentalist and composer all at the same time, in order to promote new ways and directions which put us far in advance of the function of traditional notation, change the finality of the foundations of these elements, and make us able to foresee other consequences than those contained in the uniform and unilateral elements of conventional reading.

Many of Tom Phillips' scores are actually intended to be played with a whole variety of sound sources, and require a real group strategy. Furthermore, they need not rely on technical virtuosity, and therefore find favor with non-professional musicians. The pieces by Tom Phillips thus offer the opportunity of developing means of communication of a musical nature, whose result partly depends on the conditions in place for each performance. As a consequence of their status as open works ('works in progress'), these works could well risk being defined in a much too general and vague fashion, leaving the interpreter face to face with such a great number of unknown eventualities when playing them that he would be left wandering, without points of reference, as if this process refused to grant him a foothold. This is not the case with Tom Phillips, however. By visually underlining the intended musical result, the graphic signs he invents contribute a great deal to reinforcing the identity of each process, while still granting the participants the choice of sonorous materials which can be introduced into the playing.

"Sometimes, a purely acoustic idea occurs to me, for example in a piece like *Music for n Players*, where I conceived loops of sound intertwining in time. The difficulty here was to find graphical forms equivalent to the sounds I was projecting, where the idea in the form of sound was being transfomed into graphic notation. [...] This interest of mine comes equally to the fore in a piece like *Ornamentik*, where ornament occurring in conventional notation seems to conjure up an even more imaginative world of ornament than the one which already exists, so that the interpreters are incited in turn to produce them musically. This is how I produced a graphic ensemble resulting in a score based entirely on the ornament decorating a simple line."

Tom Phillips has conducted his most meticulous plastic research in the field of notation, which effectively rids musical communication of the functionalist and overbearing aspect generally associated with the symbolic system. As in his plastic processes, his scores become tools, the consequences of which are full of promise in that they neither tend towards any sort of systemization nor seek to replace one code with another, but speculate instead on the relativity and the potential for openness inherent in all phenomena involving analysis and communication.

(London, 1979 – Fragments of an interview)

CHAPTER II

Space, architecture

Works composed by Karlheinz Stockhausen, like *Gruppen,* for three orchestras, or *Carré*, for four orchestras and four choirs positioned in such a way as to encircle the audience, are important milestones when considering the spatial dimension of writing, for they both imply a dynamic notion of musical playing which no longer necessarily depends on the conditions of Italian-style theater and its ideal conception of listening. The task of occupying space has become an integral component of the work, a factor which obliges the composer to take into consideration the architectural particularities of every hall on the occasion of each and every performance, and even to imagine spaces designed especially for the works in question.

The developments of electronics have undoubtedly encouraged investigation into the spatial qualities of sound phenomena. One of the first composers to have used electroacoustic sources in this way is Edgar Varèse who, even in his strictly instrumental works like *Hyperprisme* (1922-1923), gave an active role to the dimension of space. He writes on this topic in the article "Musique de notre temps" (Music in our Time): "In my own works, organized masses of sound evolve in opposition to each other, such that the extent and volume of sound radiation is modified during this process. By projecting sound, I am searching for the quality of a third dimension in which the sound radiation resembles light beams being swept around by a projector... in short, a continuation, a journey into space.[1]" This dimension comes to the fore especially in Iannis Xenakis' *Poème électronique*, a work

(1) — Edgar Varèse, "Musique de notre temps", in *Ecrits,* Christian Bourgois, Paris, 1983, p. 89.

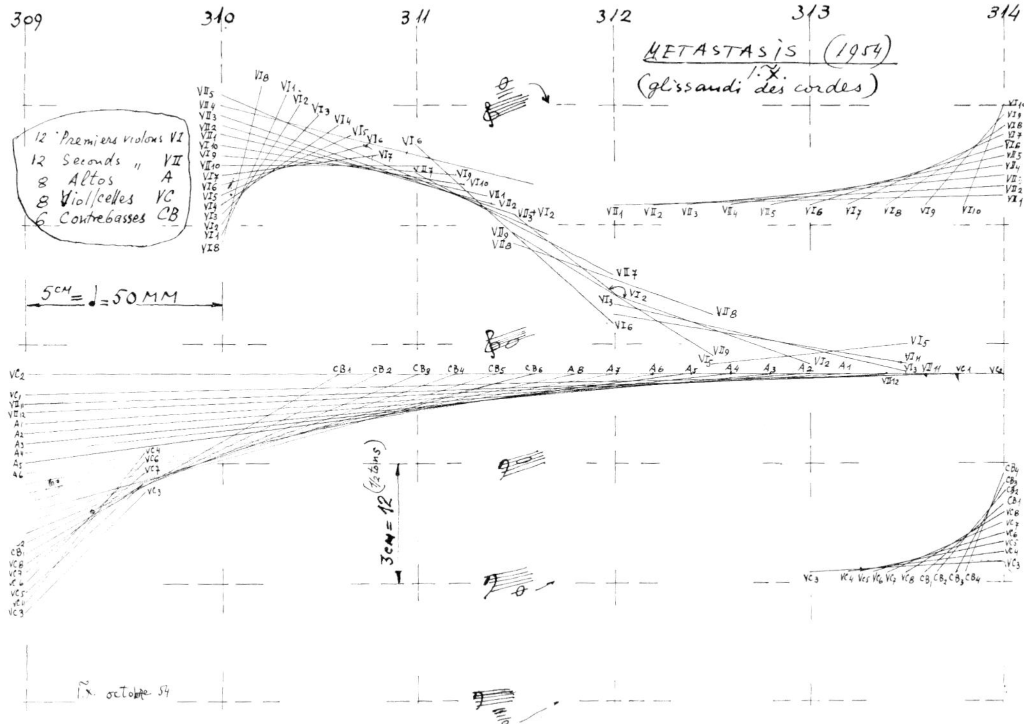

6 - Iannis Xenakis, ***Metastasis*****, 1954**
(glissandi of the strings) (**© D.R.**)

composed in the Philips laboratories in Holland. This work was intended to be amplified by means of three hundred loudspeakers set up inside the building designed by Le Corbusier and I. Xenakis for the universal exhibition in Brussels in 1958. The structure of his musical work *Metastasis* (1953-54), "the first vision of regular surfaces in sound space," in fact formed the structural basis of I. Xenakis' architectural plans for the Philips Pavilion, an edifice made of unbroken rectilinear surfaces. This project, conceived along the lines of the analogical relation which can exist between the regular surfaces of the architectural work and the combined effects of the *glissandi* of the string instruments, represents an outstanding experiment in synthesizing sound, light, and architecture, a project which itself constitutes the first stage of what I. Xenakis calls an "electronic gesture." Later works like *Diatopes* and *Polytopes* were to form decisive extensions of this research.

Polytopes is the work in which I. Xenakis succeeds best in creating phenomena where different lightings, forms existing both in time and in three-dimensional space, intersect. At the same time, this work represents the two parallel trains of thought engendered by light composition and musical composition, which converge sporadically in time, and are brought together by effects of accumulation. In the Montreal *Polytope*, for example, the continuity of the musical framework produced by four identically structured orchestras, placed at the ends of four orthogonal radii, like the spokes of a wheel, reveals itself to be relatively independent from the light show, which is essentially pointillist. I. Xenakis adheres to his principle of rigorously controlling each and every sequence of sound and light within an overall effect, which takes as much account of the planning of light trajectories as of acoustic events. The light composition on the basis of laser beams does, in fact, bear close witness to his experience in organizing sound by means of probability calculations, logical structures, group structures, and set theory.

Since the increasing complexity of temporal categories has tended to exceed the restrictive framework of concert performance and the artificial character of measured time, certain composers have found the conception of a space or a piece of architecture capable of supporting a specific musical project to be a necessary amplification of their quest to discover new reception facilities for musical practice and listening. *Dream House* by La Monte Young is one such example of a work which could be said to come to fruition within time, like a living organism "with a life and tradition of its own." In this "house of dreams," a center of meditation protected from all forms of aggression from outside, like a "dome encompassing an interior space," the music becomes inhabitable within a continuous environment of live electronic sounds, occasionally punctuated by song. Sinusoidal waves were chosen for this, because they are made up of one single frequency and therefore enable the listener to better understand the ways in which acoustic perception varies according to the zones of low and high pressure structuring an enclosed space. The movements of the audience in the hall, or the position they choose in the space, form an integral part of the initial project. Oscilloscopes are used to visualize the sound waves and their most microscopic distortions, which act as a "drone," like a continuo, for the sounds which are sung. The simultaneous visual environment created by Marian Zazeela presents light forms undergoing slow movements of mutation, where the slightest breath causes the relations between forms, lights, and projected shadows, to alter in a very fluid manner. *The Tortoise and his Dreams and Journeys*, begun in 1964, —which raises certain questions such as "the utopia of an infinite music" according to Dieter Schnebel, questions discernible as early as the work *Compositions 1960*—tends towards a type of music which eludes temporal restraints, one which is capable of "propelling itself of its own accord and without any time limit, by its own impetus alone."

François Bayle, one of the most outstanding figures of the G.R.M. (Musical Research Group), the laboratory which grew out of the Club d'Essai (Experimental Club) of the R.T.F (French Radio and Television) founded by Pierre Schaeffer, is at the root of a new method of amplifying so-called "acousmatic" acoustic sources. This involves orchestrating sound sources with a combination of several sound projectors, capable of acting as a substitute for the classic device of adding sound to images, which tends to spatialize the sound from the perimeter towards the center of the hall. Instead, this ensemble of sound projectors spreads an "orchestration" of the acoustic image outwards, in one of the most apt dimensions for propagating acoustic phenomena, whatever the shape of hall (several of François Bayle's works, like *Grande Polyphonie* dating from 1974, explore the theme of occupying space with sound in as many ways as possible). At the same period, Françoise Barrière and François Clozier were putting together the "Gmebophone" at the Center for Experimental Music in Bourges, in order to make the best of spatialized amplification of acoustic sources.

The ability to live inside of a type of music and occupy a space as if it were a "soundbox" is—independently of any predetermined spiritualistic aim—apparently the intention of Eliane Radigue in her electronic pieces. These generally appear in the form of magnetic tapes of varying duration which are combined at successive moments of synchronization during the course of indeterminate cycles. Her work on vibration and its relation to a given space includes zones of infra and ultra-sonic sounds, which are no longer intended uniquely for the faculties of hearing as such, but rather for the sensibility of the whole body. It follows, therefore, that when E. Radigue claims that "space produces its own vibrations," she is referring to space itself, which comes into play when acoustic vibrations impinge upon it.

K. Stockhausen has, for his part, experimented with the role of space on several occasions, after *Gruppen* and *Carré*, by setting his musical project in the open *(Musique dans un parc)* or by supplying the listener with the possibility of a sort of free itinerary to be traced among musical events linked to scattered locations *(Alphabet pour Liège)*, or even by helping to construct a building destined to serve as a receptacle for *Hinab-Hinauf* at the universal exhibition in Osaka. In this last case, a mobile platform was installed to enable listeners to ascend and descend on the inside of a spherical form, in which the

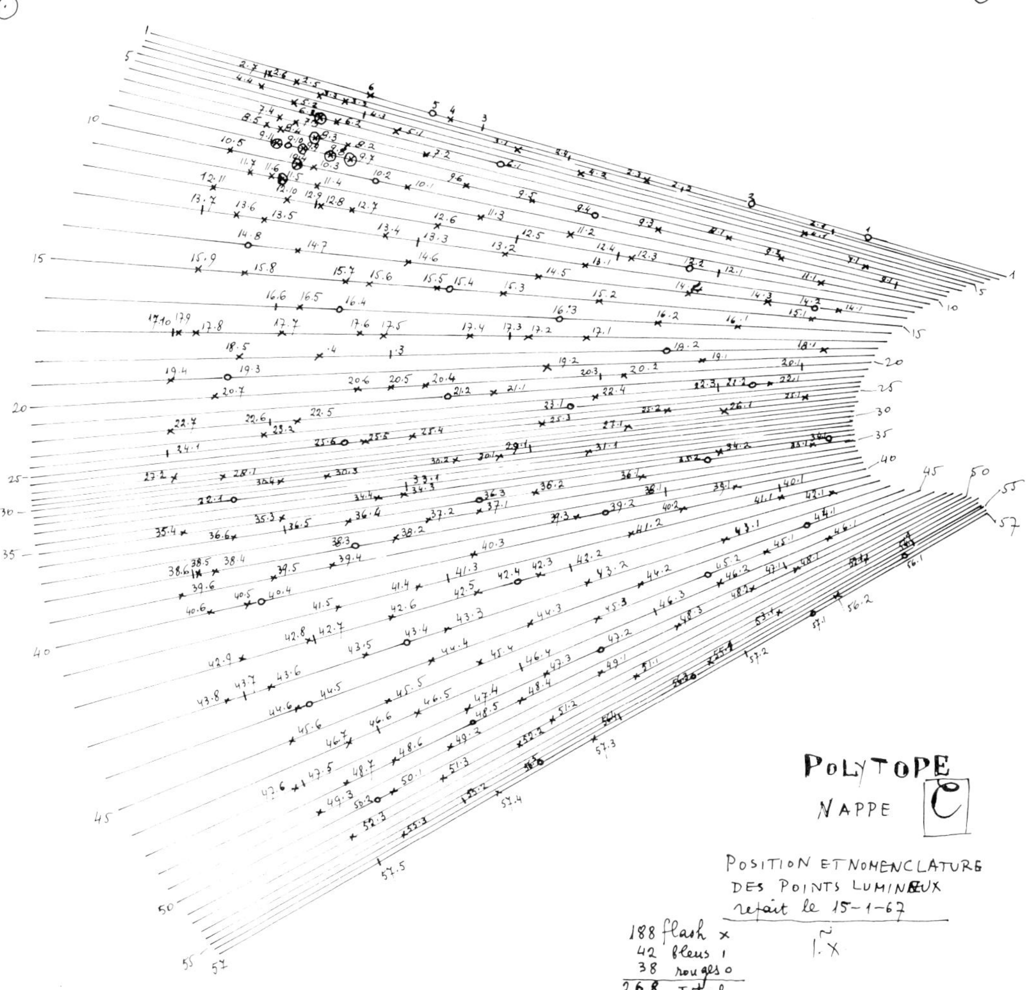

7 - Iannis Xenakis, *Polytope*, 1967
(Position and nomenclature of luminous points)
(© D.R.)

loudspeakers were situated as far apart as possible in order to facilitate the most varied acoustic trajectories as possible.

Instead of being confined to an analysis and an exploitation of its potentialities, reflection on space and architecture can take on a critical dimension, as is testified to in the work of Dorothée Selz. The theme of the series of *Références visuelles et sonores* (1973-74), which contains the piece *l'Opéra de Paris*, is in fact the cultural, social, and political links forming the core of Parisian life. Each site is treated in the form of a photographic enlargement of the façade of a building selected in advance, in which the architectural twists and turns are reworked in trompe l'œil like those of frosting applied with a cake decorator. The image obtained by this method is accompanied by a cassette giving details about the origins of the building, its function (based on documents supplied by the institution in question), and some speeches, including sound-effects or pieces of music recorded on the spot, all of which constitutes a manner of carrying out an acoustic enquiry.

More generally, it is possible today to discern the concern, harbored by composers involved in the practice of performance and installations etc., for the necessity of a more and more refined command of space corresponding to some of the most varied technical and aesthetic requirements. The amplification of electroacoustic pieces, as well as the production of scores enhancing the theatrical part of instrumental play, or even projects engaging an interaction between visual and sound elements, are generally inseparable from a spatial device created according to each case under consideration.

Iannis Xenakis

You have worked with Le Corbusier over a number of years. What benefits have you drawn from such collaboration?

My encounter with Le Corbusier occurred late in life. As far as I was concerned, architecture had ended in the 5th century B.C., notably in Athens. When I saw Le Corbusier's work, I progressively changed my mind, because his work was closely related to what I was trying to do in music, which is quite curious when you think about it. Both of us were employing ideas, seeking to organize things in such a way that aesthetic ideas entered into consideration and functioned within our work. He didn't say outright that this or that was "beautiful," but I could sense what he was aiming at in his drawings. His attitude towards the problem was similar to what I was trying to achieve. This opened my eyes to the potential meaning of visual impressions in the field of sound, and vice versa. However, at that time I was not conscious of these things, which evolved during a number of years without being expressed out loud.

Did other visual artists exert an influence on your approach?

I found Pevsner interesting because he had a conception of sculpture quite similar to mine, due to the straight lines and abstract forms he employed in his sculptures.

In other words, influence came from plastic artists working with volume, and bordering on architecture, rather than painters working in two dimensions...

I greatly appreciated Mondrian during his abstract period, but Klee less, because of the interference of figurative elements in his paintings. I didn't think much of Picasso's work either: I was conscious of the textures... conscious of the touch of his hand, his command of the medium, but this was not my main concern at that time.

Do you consider the relations you have acquired with visual arts via your architectural activities as a determining factor for your musical approach?

I think that, first and foremost, there was notation, which is visual, and confronted me with lots of problems to start with. Subsequently, drawing architectural pieces helped me a great deal. I would indeed say that I have made much use of the visual medium.

So you bridged the gap between the field of visual arts and musical notation via architecture?

Yes, architecture set me thinking about the question... of why I chose to do one thing rather than another, for example.

But some of the rough copies of your scores which I saw are graphic right from the start. Take Errikthon, *for example, with its purely visual lines. It's clear that this was only a preliminary stage of the piece, but do you do this often?*

No, it varies. Besides, these days I use graphics less and less, although I don't know why. It's possibly an error on my part, or a shortcoming, I don't know. I tend to use mathematical, or occasionally numerical types of writing etc., in which case, there are no graphics.

Nevertheless, didn't your experience with UPIC, *for example, give you an incentive to develop relations between sounds and graphic signs...*

No, I don't think so.

... or to experiment with connections between certain types of graphics and certain types of sounds?

No, but this did oblige me to give some thought to certain things. Why, for example, do I choose to go through the graphics stage before transforming this into music? I have now understood that there are certain structures contained in visual and auditory experience that are comparable,—mental structures, to be precise. For example, time, so fundamental in music, is marked by a succession of ordered instants, as it were, in that they occur one after the other. The points along a straight line are organized in the same way. It is quite easy, therefore, to transfer from one to the other. The same goes for pitches, as these are also ordered sets which can be written on a straight line, unlike frequencies, which are a little more complicated, being curves.

The *glissando* is a straight line slanted in space. If we were to define the *glissando,* we would have to say that it is pitch and time rolled into one. The points marking time and pitch are ordered, which means they can be transcribed onto an oblique straight line.

But weren't you at all hindered by certain symbolic conventions in traditional musical notation, when the very types of events you are resorting to tend to leave such conventions behind?

Yes, of course, this is a hindrance. It's essential to know the limits of every type of writing. In any case, there are even limits in graphic writing, whether it be numerical, graphic, or traditional.

Is this the reason why you sometimes resort to a transitional stage, between your idea and the score, operating via the intermediary of graphics?

Yes, I sometimes do this in the form of notes or sketches, in order to preserve the character of the idea I had at a given moment, that's all...

In your oeuvre, there are some experiences which fundamentally testify to the encounter between elements of sound and vision, in Diatopes *and* Polytopes, *to name but two.*

Yes, in this case the two types of experience run parallel to one another, because I am very attracted to visual things. In the visual and auditory fields, there are ideas and structures which can compare with each other on a higher plane than the one I talked about in terms of points on a straight line. For example, masses of sound events or masses of visual events (the points which fall into line or vanish all together) are similar from the point of view of their structure and their treatment. They can be treated in the same way, and with the same principles if, of course, one takes into consideration the phenomena of time etc., which are not at all easy to assimilate.

On this very point, could you say where the possibilities for comparing visual and sound phenomena begin, and where they end?

I'll give you an example. A circle is a line that bites its own tail, which joins up with itself. If we interpret this in terms of sound, we have to take pitch, the simplest sound property of all, and draw a two-dimensional circle, with pitch and time represented by its axes. If you start from a given point of the circle, and trace the circle from the lowest to the highest point, you then begin to descend. However, at a given moment, you must inevitably start going backwards in terms of time, at which point it is no longer possible to advance. Therefore, if we want to obtain an auditory circle, it should really resemble a sinusoid.

In which case, you would make alterations...

Yes, of course.

In Polytopes, *I have the impression that you have preserved a certain independence between different levels, so that there is no analogy between the fields of vision and sound.*

I agree, because these are two distinct ways of proceeding which don't require to be linked together. Human beings are intelligent enough to be able to follow two messengers at a time.

But is this also due to the fact that you had the impression that the two modes of perception were somewhat heterogeneous?

Yes, of course, as there is an element of heterogeneity whenever we see and hear music. For example, when we see a singer singing, we listen to what is sung from a musical point of view, and this has nothing to do with the singer's appearance, which is quite independent.

And this is precisely what you did when you composed Polytopes, *you created two separate types of discourse...*

Exactly. Occasionally, there are some compositions, or structures, which coincide, as for example in the *Diatope* presented at the Pompidou Center. For the inaugural performance, there were one thousand six hundred electronic flashes which I was free to trigger off as I wished. This provided a sort of mass of luminous points, like sound points. When working with space, I have at my disposal two dimensions, or three, plus time. In music I can have more than one dimension by changing, for example, timbres in relation to pitch. With timbres this provides two dimensions and, with time, three, including intensity. This gives me a total of three dimensions, plus time. However, it is important to take care not to assimilate these dimensions in a simplistic manner, because the way in which our eyes and ears intercept visual or sound phenomena is quite different.

On this point, have you been tempted to reflect upon previous experiments which have revealed certain limits or, alternatively, certain new opportunities?

Yes, in this case, one tends to follow one's instinct and imagination, and it is felt, even without being conscious of the limits, that there is an underlying thought which actually does the work for us—on another plane, thankfully.

Are there any examples of links between the fields of vision and sound which have left you with a particularly strong impression, without having necessarily originated in your imagination?

No, I don't think so, unless I were to express myself like Debussy on the subject of wind in the trees. He heard the wind and saw the leaves moving, which amounted to a complete, total phenomenon. The sea, all the phenomena we see in nature, rain, hail, even sand in one's eyes, such natural phenomena usually formed the origin of such impressions... When I was taking part in demonstrations against the Nazis in Athens during the occupation, there was a genuine sound chaos, with shouts resulting from the Germans' shooting into the crowd. I was at the front the whole time and I was aware of the danger of being hit, but at the same time I was listening to what was going on. This is something which reappeared later in my work. It is, therefore, both a social and acoustic phenomenon, highly complex. It is also what led me later on to use probability calculation (although at that time I didn't even know that such calculation existed, as I was young and never gave it a thought) on the basis of the memory of former impressions, and of events parallel to others, like that of clouds of mosquitoes.

How did you come to establish the intersection of visual and sound elements as found in Polytopes?

I had designed the Philips Pavilion in Brussels in 1958. There, they performed a piece by Varèse and one by myself. On top of this, there was a visual show, thought up by Le Corbusier, based on fixed images taken from his architecture and architecture in general, with all sorts of imagery, realist for the most part. I was astonished to see that the images weren't more abstract, as his painting was relatively abstract, after all.

Apart from natural phenomena, I had no recourse to representations which could have incited me to do this. But when I was much younger, I had written a study on one of Aeschylus' tragedies and I had then imagined visually the procedure I had to follow. This wasn't all that extraordinary, but it did appeal to my imagination insofar as it interested me to do something with my eyes. It goes without saying that the proximity to Le Corbusier and the phenomenon of architecture increased this preoccupation. I learnt to see things better than before.

Though in fact, didn't the curves of the Philips Pavilion depend on Metastasis?

Certainly. When drawing, I had sketched a lot of straight lines which intermingled, knocked into each other, and I asked myself why didn't I write the *glissandi* in the same fashion. Afterwards, I composed *Metastasis* on the basis of straight lines, in which the "regular forms" were shells made up of straight lines that shifted in space.

Did you follow up this approach afterwards, this sort of transfer of curves, and of straight lines, which subsequently enter into architectural forms?

I don't think so, but I did develop rhythms of elements like "pieces of undulatory glass" at the Tourette convent, as elsewhere, for example... also in India. At that time I was preoccupied by the problem of rhythm in music and I transferred my know-how to the field of architecture, which was not the done thing at that time. I set standards based on distances in dynamic relations, which meant geometric relations in the case of music, likewise in the case of time, because I realized that we were rather more familiar with the geometric evolution of durations than with additive or arithmetic ones. In this respect, the "golden section" was both at the same time. There were also all the elements which relate to mass: each unity of length had a particular density and contained a fixed number of points. In the case of architecture, this would correspond to the façade, and in music to the question of time and rhythm, both residing in a high density which could decrease, or reduce to almost nothing, then start all over again, a process which provided one way, among others, of playing with densities. These are notions which have actually existed in traditional music since time immemorial, but which had not previously received prime attention.

These are therefore mathematical operations and calculations which allowed you to imagine relations generating sound out of visual material?

Yes, and vice versa. There were visual phenomena which demanded more abstract solutions, then others, the ideas.

What led you to the experiments carried out with the UPIC?

When I began the drawings in preparation for *Metastasis,* I thought that if only I had access to a system which could translate musical ideas directly without me having to rack my brains writing notes, that's all... This is an idea which weighed upon me for years, until technology came to my rescue.

Did this benefit you personally, and your own ideas. Did it help you to put forward new hypotheses? I ask this because a great deal of composers have worked on the UPIC.

That's difficult to say. I don't think so.

So all this has been a dream for you...

But I did all this for others, not just for myself. I thought it could be useful, and I was excited by the possibility of experimenting with a machine which didn't yet exist, and seeing what could be made of it. This research is not over yet, either, because all depends on the complexity and refinement of the technology.

But the UPIC is nevertheless fundamentally different from the graphic notations invented by composers like John Cage or Earle Brown in the fifties?

They do have something in common though, because both amount to artistic gestures. Of course, gestures can be psychological or correspond to a completely different intention, but they can also be precise when it comes to drawing a sound movement. In this respect, gestures are transformed into sound more directly than if they pass through the intermediary of an interpreter, for example.

The strange fact remains, however, that you have never resorted to graphic notation...

No, because I think that if a composer has something to say, he should go the whole hog and say it. If the composer puts someone in-between his imagination and what he wants to hear, this creates a filter. This might work, or it might not. In general, this person, the filter, has an education behind him, and tends, therefore, to reproduce just the things which are familiar to him, and nothing more.

Whereas the UPIC is a graphic notation designed with the composer in mind...

Precisely. At his desk, the composer can create sound structures he hears, and subsequently experiment by switching from one place to another. This means he can improvise quite easily, for example by changing the order of sequences, or by modifying other parameters.

You have treated space extensively in your oeuvre. Did you do so solely from a musical point of view, or from a visual point of view as well?

Both. In *Terretektohr*, for example, I had in mind the form of a spiral. A spiral can only be obtained with a single line. If, from the qualitative point of view, the colors are changed, the spiral is lost. As a result, it was imperative to install only one type of instrument all around, on the periphery, and I chose the strings. Then came the question of time, because a spiral suspended in space is one thing, but it requires time to give it meaning. Sounds have to be perceived one after the other and traced with the ear, not with the eyes. Our eyes indicated that the musicians were scattered around, arranged as points in space, and more or less forming a ring, but this is not what inter-

A HOUSE

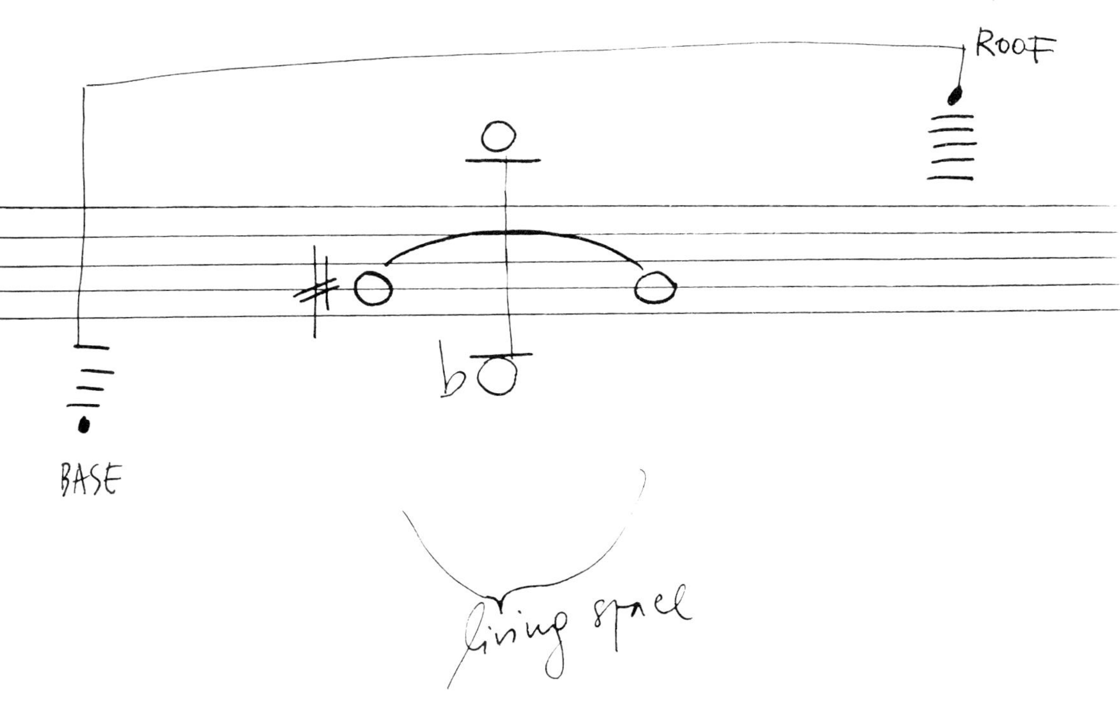

8 - Milan Knizak, *A House*, 1965
(© D.R.)

ested me. A spiral is something which revolves, twirling towards a center which is simultaneously unfurling. Therefore, in order to find a temporal or spatial equivalent, it was necessary to play on speed, as with something which turns faster and faster. There you have it, these are the analogies I'm exploring.

Have you developed any others, in other works?

Yes, for example, I have transposed group structures into space and into the field of timbre—group structures which are either concomitant, or independent from each other. One must constantly take care that the whole remains perceptible, however. Perceptible for whom, you may ask? For the composer? The latter is liable to make mistakes. Perceptible for the listener, therefore, but which listener? The question remains open.

Do you think there exists a danger of imposing one system of logic on another while disregarding the level of perception...

Of course, this danger always exists. This is what happened to serial music.

In other words, it works on paper, but not in listening practice.

Not quite. I would say that it could work eventually, but without arousing any interest from outside. From the point of view of the sound, on the other hand, a dynamic effect is a prerequisite, or else the whole thing seems absurd.

The appropriate equivalent between the form you choose, and its embodiment in a sound therefore has to be found...

That's right. It has to mean something from the point of view of the sound, even if the form has nothing to do with what you can hear. It is essential that the form incites an interest in the sounds that can be heard.

Have you ever had ideas for a visual structure for which you could find no equivalent musical expression?

Possibly.

Perhaps your ideas have been jointly acoustic and *visual, which is why you haven't been confronted with this problem...*

Yes, though if I have a sound-related idea which extends into a visual idea and vice versa, it is only momentary. The transition from ideas to the realization of a piece causes things to fade, little by little. In the course of this necessary progression, one often loses the element of magic. One day you have dazzling ideas, and two days later you look at what you've acheived and say: "What the heck is that?" After all, this is how a composer matures.

(Paris, April 16, 1992)

CHAPTER III

Plastic Contributions to the Musical Experience

Composers have not failed to play on the visual impact of their scores, particularly since the rise of graphic notation; numerous plastic artists (especially those who practice collage) have made use in their own way of this coded space for specific signs, destined to remain partially secret for the non-initiate. Thus fragments of scores, completely detached from any lingering idea of a later interpretation, intervene in certain collages by Robert Motherwell, Jiri Kolar, and Ladislav Novak. Such borrowings sometimes take on the value of an homage to a particular composer or work, notably with Dominique Thiolat.

Jannis Kounellis frequently stages his paintings in association with musical performances or dance actions, proceeding for example by enlarging scores which are generally covered over in a gradual manner, such that parts of them are hidden, as if memory had slipped away—unless the imagination should come to fill the gaps and prolong the construction manifested by the organization of the notations in space.

The concept of "*musica visiva*" (visual music) originates with Luciano Ori. His score-collages do not represent a visual transcription of impressions received upon hearing a piece of music, nor any interpretation thereof. "The transgression of the genre 'music' is total," for this visual music seeks to be another music, a different kind of music. "To hear it you need merely look, and to see it, just listen"; any attempt at interpretation is simply reductive.

Partnerships between painters and composers in the elaboration of scores in book form remain relatively rare. One may cite the case of John Furnival's work with Hugh Davies, where the graphic and musical aspects are closely associated; for my part, I have contributed to several score-books, in particular with Aldo Mondino, Tom Phillips, Claude Melin, Jan Voss, and François Dilasser.

If the transmission of music largely takes place through the intermediary of the score—at least where schooled Western music is concerned—one must nonetheless underline the fact that sheet music is today but one visual support of musical culture among others. Many objects potentially contain music, beyond, of course, musical instruments themselves. This is notably the case with records. Here though, we must distinguish between the use of the record as a strictly plastic object—which is therefore rendered mute—and its simultaneous exploitation on both the acoustic and visual levels. In most of the works involving records there appears a subversive intent with regard to the phenomenon of the record as a consumer object dedicated solely to furnishing as faithful a reproduction as possible of recorded music, and thus calling for what is, in sum, a passive attitude.

As early as 1924, Laszlo Moholy-Nagy published the article "The New Creation in Music—the Possibilities of the Phonograph" in the journal *Der Sturm*; the same year, Kurt Schwitters recorded an excerpt of his *Ursonate*, joined to issue 13 of the journal *Merz – Grammophonplatte*. In 1936, Edgar Varèse carried out his first experiments with records. The beginnings of concrete music in 1948, through the initiative of Pierre Schaeffer, are linked to the manipulation of the same support.

From the late fifties on, many records have been realized by plastic artists, notably Yves Klein (*Musique du vide*, in 1959), Jean Dubuffet (*Expériences musicales*, in 1961), then Karl Appel, Henning Christiansen, Camille Bryen, Joseph Beuys, Ben, Bernar Venet, Tom Phillips, Wolf Vostell, Hermann Nitsch, Milan Grygar... Occasionally, artists have worked in collaboration with composers (Gavin Bryars realized a version of *Irma*, an opera conceived by Tom Phillips). The acoustic

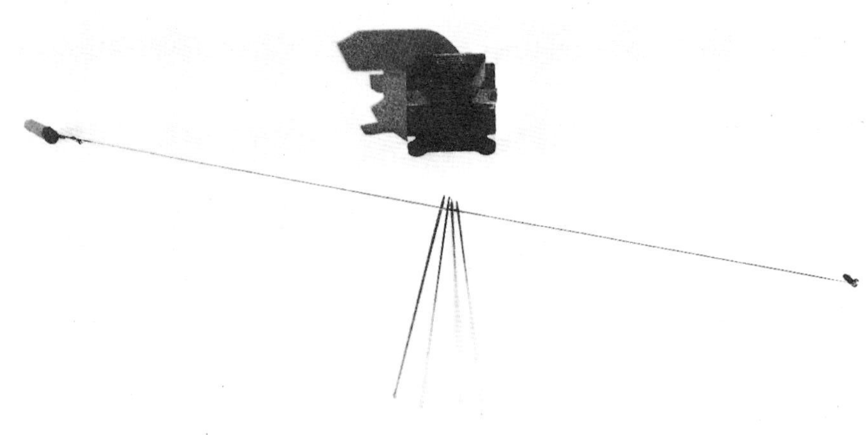

9 - Takis, *Sculpture musicale*, 1965
(© D.R.)

support is at times a cassette, as in the case of Dieter Roth, who has frequently incorporated cassettes within his plastic works and installations.

Even if it is destined to remain silent, the record or magnetic tape bears the trace of concrete moments, which are "stored up" within it. Thus in Sarkis' work, the spectator's attention is drawn to magnetic tape as a virtual reservoir of music, and this in a manner which is both musically and historically very precise (for example, works by composers of the Vienna school in *La Fin des Siècles, le Début des Siècles*, 1984). The accumulations of tape that Sarkis includes in many of his *Scènes* are seemingly charged with temporal experiences. In the words of Elvan Zabunyan, "by recording it on magnetic tape, Sarkis renders Time visible—through the length of the recording, and thus of the tape. Sarkis also plays on the time of recording... There is a very close relationship between lived time and the visual length of this time.[1]" In the very first works where magnetic tape was used, in 1973, one can already see Sarkis' approach to this notion of measure. He recorded a word or a phrase, cut out the section of recorded tape, and inscribed it with the word or the phrase; thus one obtained visually, according to the length of the tape, the duration of the word pronounced and recorded.

Distortion, dismantling, and dissection: such are the fates frequently reserved for sound supports (whether musical instruments or records) in the production of a certain number of artists, notably at the time of Fluxus and Nouveau Réalisme. The object in question seems destined to return definitively to silence[2] after having undergone all kinds of trials by force—as witnessed in numerous sculptures by Arman—or even a softening operation, as in Claes Oldenburg's *Ghost Drum Set* of 1972 (the same artist had previously imagined a "soft drum kit" as a concert hall for London's Battersea Park).

On the contrary, other artists choose to take advantage of the

(1) — Catalogue of the Sarkis exhibition, Le Magasin, Centre d'Art Contemporain de Grenoble, 1992, p. 9.
(2) — As Christian Dotrement said, "Music is the poor man's silence."

plastic potential implied in certain instruments. This is the case of Catherine Arnaud and the player piano. C. Arnaud herself fabricates the instrument's rolled scores, made in the form of grids with perforations corresponding to different notes. She retraces these grids on the strip of paper constituting the painting. Placed above the piano, the painting is sectioned into six horizontal strips which represent the total length of the roll. This approach seeks to bring the structural properties of a musical sequence into visual relief, even while sticking as close as possible to the support which generates the acoustic phenomenon.

Certain artists play with the entire gamut of actions that can be based on the supports of musical culture. Such is the case of Milan Knizak, who since the early sixties has engaged in a quasi-systematic exploration of the visual and acoustic resources offered by the record groove and today by the compact disk, obtaining results that naturally incline him now toward musical activity, now toward plastic art.

Milan Knizak

What are the principle stages in your work with sound and the plastic arts?

The first art, or better, the first medium I used was music; I was about 11 or 12 when I started to compose songs, simple pop songs, influenced by songs from before the war. A little later, when I was about 13, I composed jazz music, which I think is not too bad. I made only a few compositions. Some are recorded, and I think they are full of strange disharmony, which is "para-natural" for me: I must be born with it. As a kid, I also liked chamber music because it's very clear, it's beautiful, and I could read it. Then I started to write, and started to be interested in the visual media. I worked with them, and I studied; I didn't do much music because I didn't have the time. Around 1963 I bought a record player, but I only had a very few records which I played all the time, and it became boring. I wanted to make the music more interesting, so I said, all right, I'll play them slow, I'll play them fast; and when that wasn't enough, then I started to break them, to scratch them. That was the beginning of my "broken music" project. It was very funny, this music: maybe I was aggressive to the records, but the music was not aggressive, it was more like—funny, optimistic. It was nice for me, a nice experience to find out that music, even if it's turned down, broken, destroyed, whatever, is still music, it still has some kind of expression. It was very important for me. Unfortunately these old records are all gone (maybe there is one in the collection of Hanns Sohm, in Germany) because they were all old, very fragile records.

A little later I had a band, which was like a rock'n'roll band, but not really. Some people said it was the first punk music in the world; maybe so. It was very simple, very hard, short and hard texts, pushy. After those songs I wrote for the group, I started to work, because it was a bad time in Czechoslovakia. I had come back from the States, and it was a very closed, isolated situation for me because of the politics. So I began seriously working with architecture. For me, architecture and music are very closely related. In the early 70s, I began "switching media." Briefly said, it means that "I played a house, and I built a song." It's easily possible: if you take a "three-axes system," then one axis is the length of the tone, the other, the height, and the third, the dynamic. With these three you can build an object or an architecture, and vice-versa—which was a very good experience for me. Of course, I couldn't play buildings because I didn't have a computer at that time, so it was impossible; but I played cubes, small stuff. With a computer it's easily possible to switch these media any time.

But it was an excellent experience for me: music as architecture. I thought about music and architecture in the same way, and from that I drew many compositions which are more like structures, simple buildings, walls (I call them "walls").

But you had to invent your own rules to go from an architectural structure to a musical structure...

10 - **Sarkis, *La Danseuse*, 1987**
(in the hammam of Saint Sophie, built by the architect Sinan; marble, magnetic tape, drums covered with gold leaves)
(© D.R.)

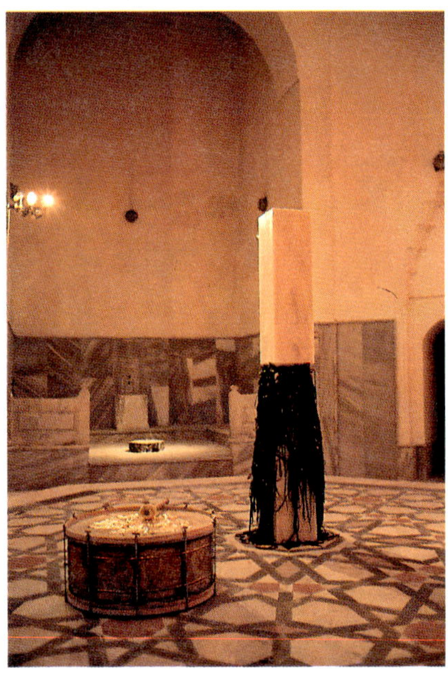

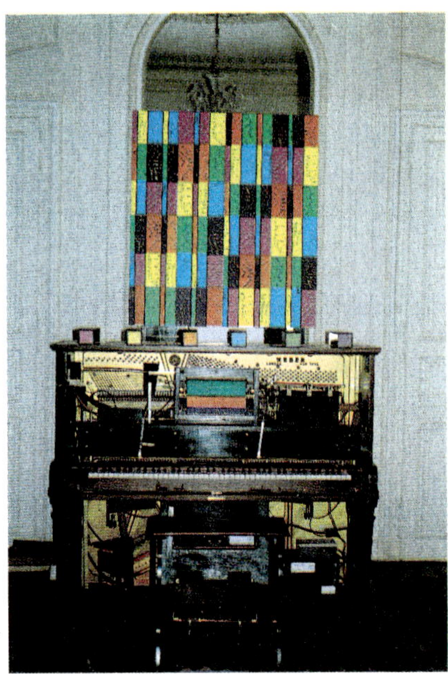

11 - **Catherine Arnaud, *Variations d'après un thème de J.S. Bach*, 1989**
(Acrylic on clothed cardboard 100 x 124).
7-meter-long player-piano roll corresponding to the musical score on the above picture, 3-minute-long musical piece.
(© D.R.)

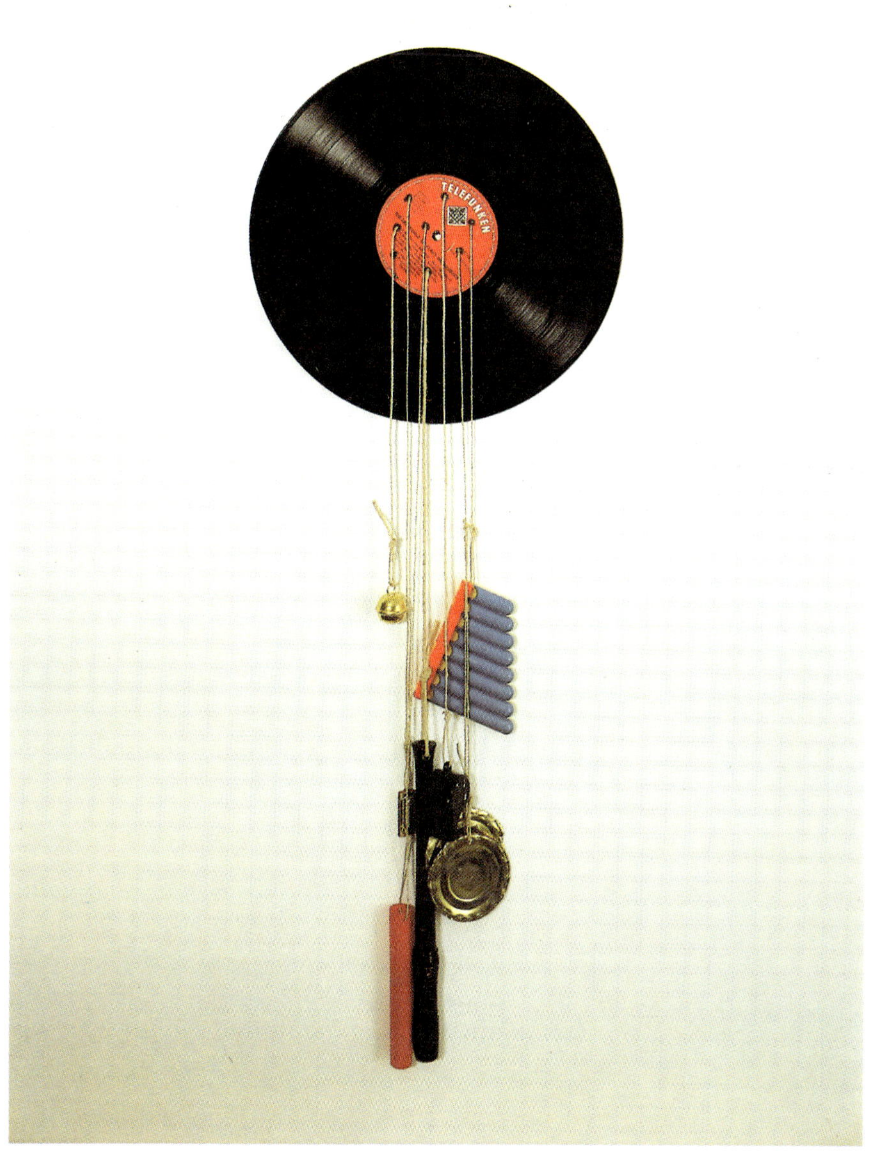

12 - Milan Knizak, ***Untitled*****, 1963-1985** ('broken music')
(© D.R.)

Not really. I used ready-made material in music, and ready-made material in architecture. It's all there. Take a fugue by Bach—it's the best building that you'll ever find, the structure is unbelievable. I was even taking compositions by Mozart and others; for part of the composition I said "this is a house," "this is a room," because for me it was a house, a room, or a wall. I found it there, it was already there, I didn't have to invent it, it was there. I just used it. Duchamp took the urinal or the bottle drier and said "this is a fountain and this is a sculpture." Of course it was not a sculpture, it was a bottle drier, but it became a sculpture because he said so. Potentially, being a sculpture was already in it, but nobody saw it before. It means, these architectural elements were in the music already, or the musical elements were in the architecture already. I was also studying mathematics at that time, and then I used mathematic formulas for music. I used all the technical media coming from architecture, mathematics, geometry, or whatever, for music.

Maybe it was more conceptual than anything else, but for me it was a great experience, and since that time, I have always been almost sure I can switch anything with anything; maybe because I experienced that with my own body, with my own senses, with my own fingers. It's difficult to understand, but it's possible sometimes to look at your bed like at your dog, or to look at your hat like at an airplane. Then if you switch these meanings, you always find something new that way, because you confront your experience of the object or the phenomenon with the new reality. This led me to another stage of music which I called "thought music" or "intuitive music"—music that was impossible to play, impossible to hear, you could only imagine it. If you say, for example, "there is music hidden in your fingernail," there's music in your fingernail, for sure, but you can't hear it, you can just think about it, you can only imagine how it sounds. Does music have to sound? I don't know... It's the kind of question which interests me all the time. Maybe it's possible to define music, but for me, I didn't want to define music exactly, because in my work I'm always using media without asking about the differences between the media. I can use a visual art piece—an abstract work—or a music piece, or a piece of architecture, or a written text, anything, without asking whether it's better or different; I just ask if it's necessary in that moment. I always use music as a very special medium, because it's so very abstract; for me, it's like something secret. Music has something you can't touch: it comes and goes, and maybe it leaves some tracks on you, inside of you, but you can't touch it, even if you have it on your record or somewhere in your synthesizer. It comes always differently because you are in a different mood... Now let's come back to the situation in the 70s when I started to use my records as visual pieces. I used many records in my last few installations, just to show that even if the record is destroyed, even if it's impossible to play it, you still are aware of the record as a record, as something on which music was, as just a kind of holder for music. And you think about it like something which had music inside, even if the music is not there, even if you can't play it: you show the records, which are almost impossible or completely impossible to play, you don't play them, but the music is present. This is the way I like it: with your visual reception, you *look* at the music, you don't hear it. You look at it, and you have it, and you know about it, which is beautiful.

The idea of using records like that came very late, in the 80s, long after the "broken music" project. At the same time, I have always continued writing music in the form of scores—for example, chamber music scores for quartets, or compositions for very few instruments. It's very classical in a way, but using all the different experiences I had through many long years of this "broken music": all sorts of music, jazz, folk, and recently, pop songs. I also gave a few concerts with music I had already recorded: I had "broken records," I had tapes with my pre-recorded music, with my "ready pieces" which were already recorded before, and I had keyboards. It was like playing with an orchestra: I was using my own material to create a new piece. I could also use the material of other people, it's not a problem, I did that too, but I prefer to use my own material like new material.

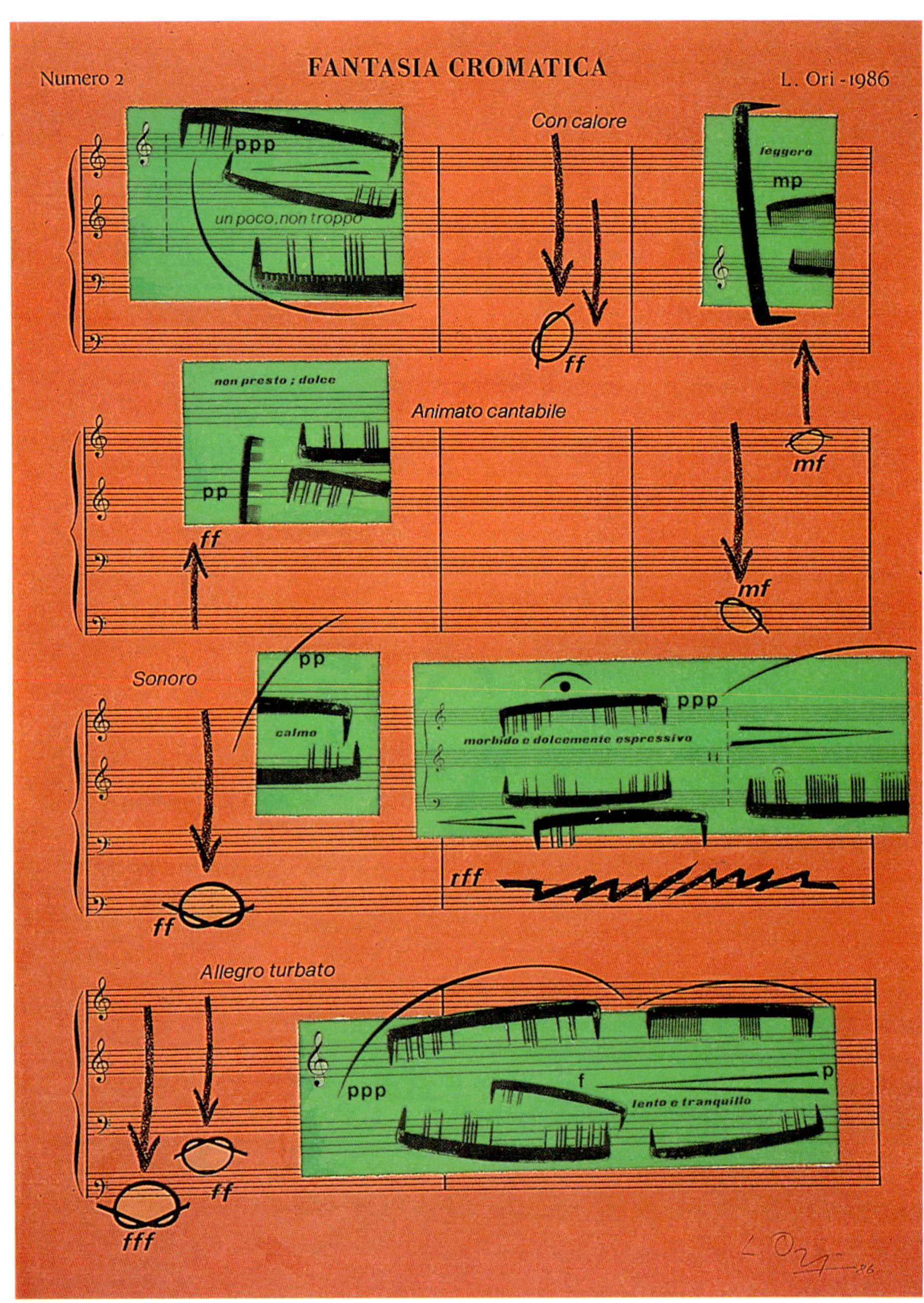

13 - Luciano Ori, *Fantasia Cromatica*, 1986
(70 x 50 cm - mixed technique)
(© D.R.)

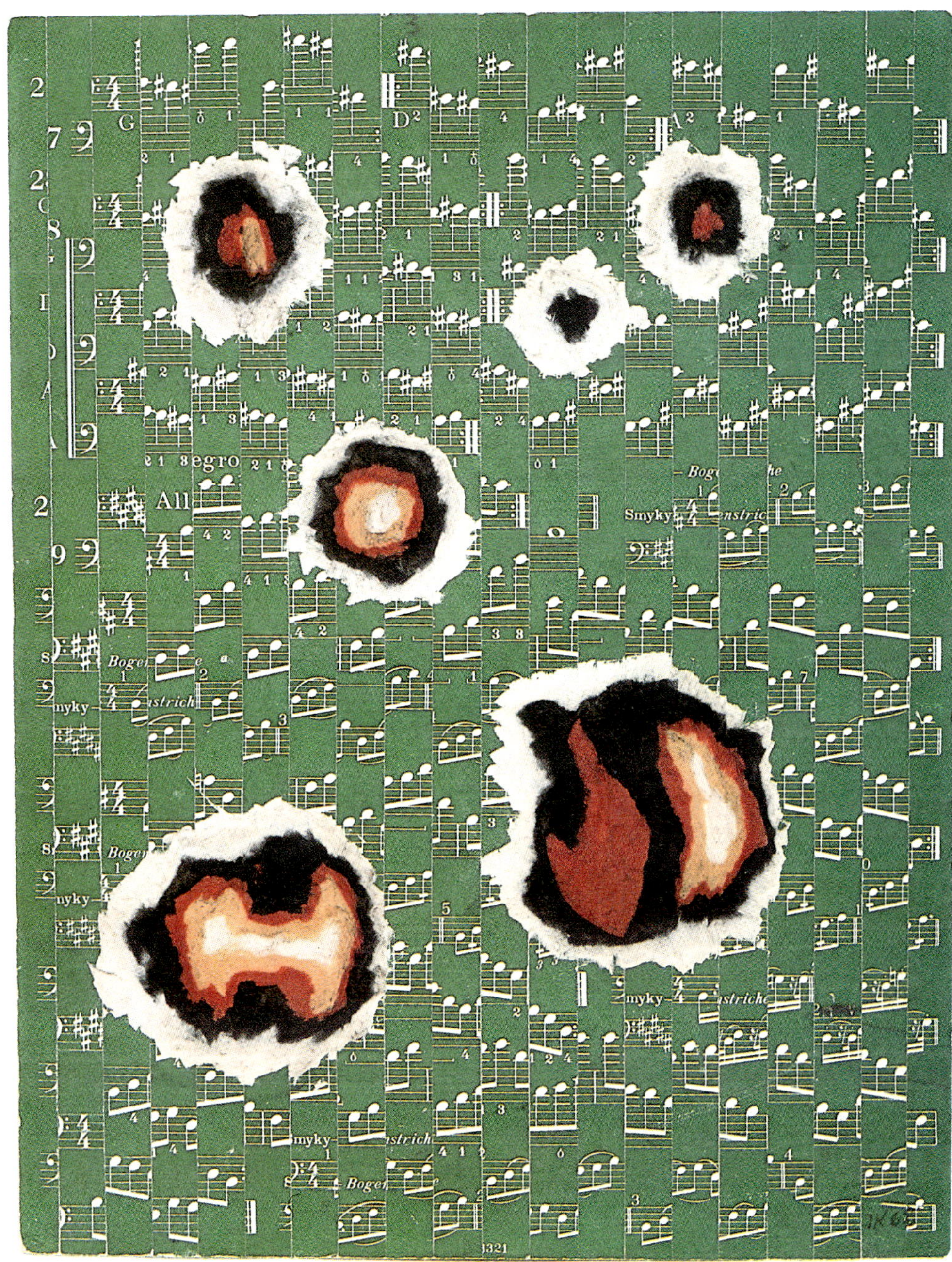

14 - Jiri Kolar, ***Smyky*****,1963**
photo by Gaël Leroux

But you use also pre-existing scores, cutting them, for instance.

Right. That project started at the end of the 60s, together with the "broken music." I used folk songs, but I changed the score. And then I began using any kind of score, putting together a new composition out of existing compositions by other people, writing "in it," i.e. changing the tunes, or just using it as raw material: it was cut down, I used it completely differently, and you couldn't recognize the old piece (unless I wanted the old piece to be recognized). I did many scores in that way. I once did it very mechanically, cutting it or maybe just putting a pause in between, or using just very few notes, very few sounds out of the whole composition. But I also did it by putting the material very carefully together, like a real composition. I use all the possibilities: pieces without a musical sense, just mechanically arranged—which also has a careful musical sense—and carefully composed works. It's the same with my "broken music": I sometimes did very rough combinations, for instance when I cut the records, but sometimes also very careful combinations.

Do you just choose the way you are going to compose at the last minute, or do you have a system?

No, I have a system, of course. Sometimes, I did it just rough, with what I found. But sometimes I was looking for something special, like composing a certain kind of a song together with a certain kind of music: maybe brass music together with opera, with a soprano solo. Then I needed some kind of rock'n'roll, or some rhythm and blues music, so I went looking for those records, and I composed them. But I want to try all the variety of different things: from very mechanical, very accidental things all the way to very careful mixtures.

Is collage a very important notion for you?

I guess so. But collage, for me, it's collage of anything. I can put together my hair, water, and sound. This is also a collage for me. But maybe I would not call it a collage, because a collage is something which is flat in visual art. For me collage is more like a juxtaposition, putting things or phenomena together; they don't have to come from the same media. I did it many times, in many different fields of my work, putting together things that were never put together before. I find these connections always very useful. It's the same with music, or with architecture. And I think collage is gorgeous. The idea of collage is good, because each element brings its own meaning, and gains another meaning in the piece. Every collage has at least two levels of meaning, which is very good: then you can make many different levels. Therefore collage is a kind of magic for me. About three years ago I started a project called *Double Scores*. I carried out a series of them last year in Germany, using pieces of broken records or compact disks which I placed like notes in the score. It means that you can read the score which is made out of pieces of records —having music inside them—and you can play the score according to the position of the "notes" on the staves. I made about twenty collages like that.

Do you try to determine very precise relationships between the visual aspects and the sound aspects, or do you let things go and interpenetrate?

The second, the second! I don't see much difference between the media. It would be very nice if things could just flow into each other, although it's sometimes very difficult. For me, first of all, sound is very natural, because you have sound everywhere. To live without a sound is almost impossible. It means that there is no piece which is completely for your eyes. If you go into a museum, people are there: even if you don't listen, they give you a sort of background. You never look at anything without sound—so the next step is just to take it and underline it, use it purposefully. I'm not somebody who always combines, like some people who always make installations with paintings, or put objects and music together. I don't do that. I respect it, but for me it's a little too artificial. I just like to use music, or to find music in almost anything. I do music, and a certain kind of music must be produced together with the visual elements, as I showed in some compositions where musicians had to be placed in

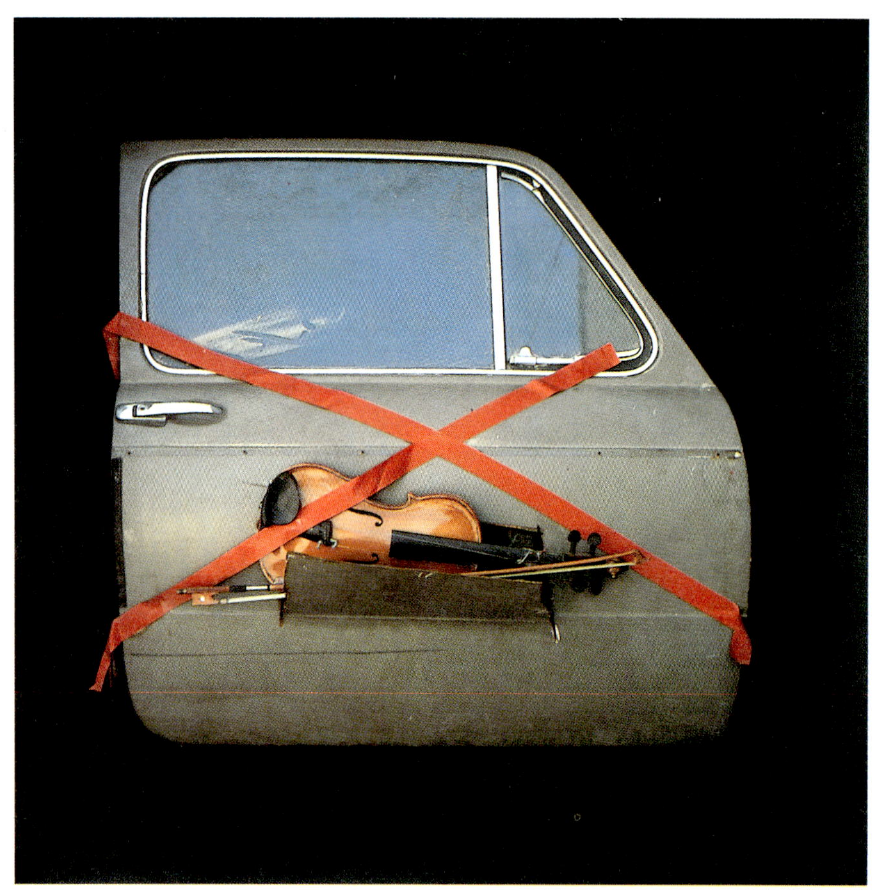

15 - Wolf Vostell, *El Fandango*, 1986
(137,5 x 38,5 cm - Hispania series; Plexiglass objects)
photo by Galerie Lavignes, Paris **(© D.R.)**

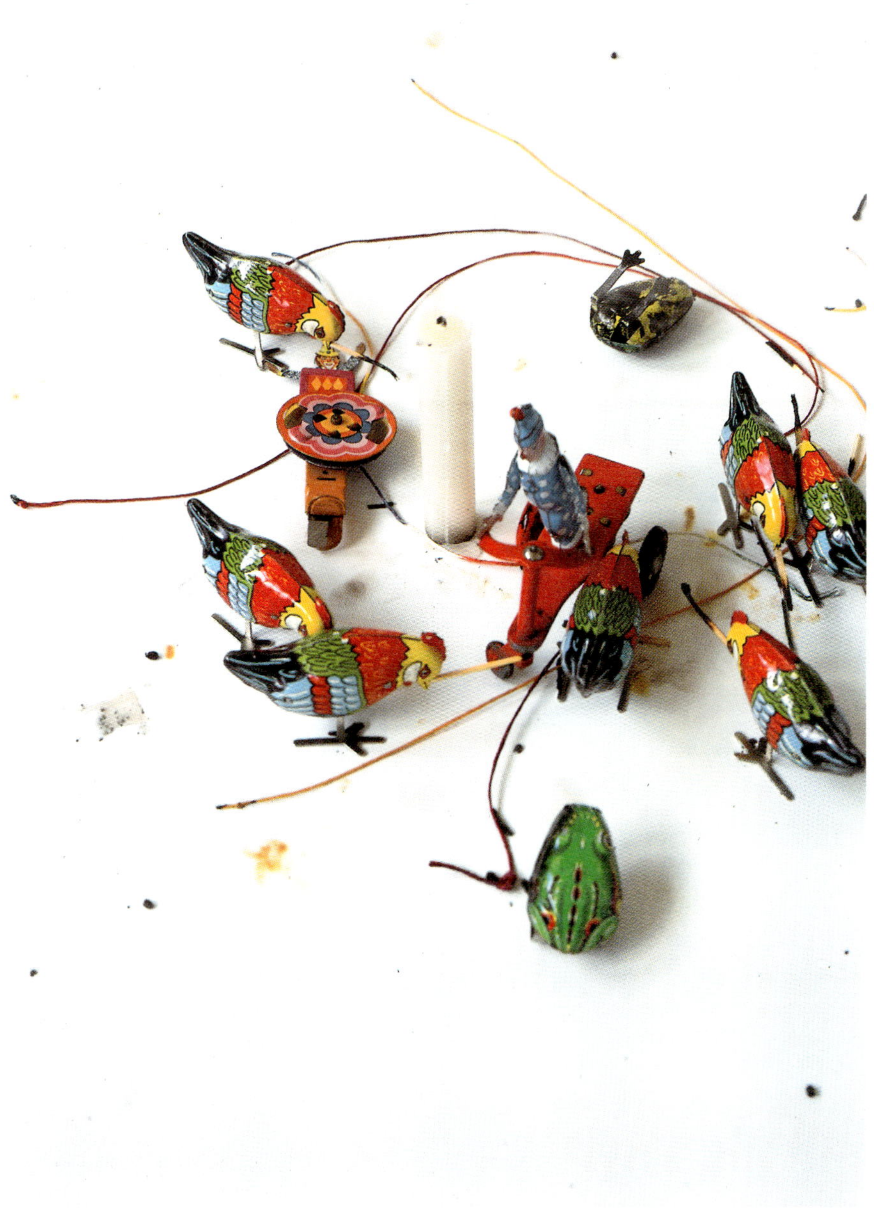

16 - Milan Grygar,
Living Drawing carried out by Mechanical Objects, 1991
(102 x 73 cm - paper)
photo by Stefan Grygar
(© D.R.)

special spots because I wanted the sound to come from a certain place, or where the listeners were placed in the middle or somewhere; but mostly I'm just making music which has the visual part already in it, like in a score, or from an object like a record, which is a visual piece too. The music is on it, but it's also a visual piece because you can't record music without some kind of a holder. If the music comes from that holder and you have it in your hand—like your doorbell—then it's a visual piece. It means that music is very abstract, but we are not able to realize that it's really abstract, we always put it together with some kind of an instrument, whether technical or not. For me, it's natural that the system of music is very abstract, but it must come from somewhere. And thus it comes from you, from a human being (the voice), or from a musical instrument, or from a technical instrument; but it's always connected with something material. I like to imagine music which possibly exists separately. Music *is* abstract, but to make it, we have to use something very real; that's maybe the bridge between music and human beings.

And you play on these kinds of ambiguities?

Right. I did a few pieces where visual pieces and sound pieces worked together. But it's not typical for my work. For me, the music is present in the visual piece, or the visual piece is present in music, and very seldom are they divided. That's the way I do it all the time. The bridge between visual art and music is very tight, it's very solid and natural. Maybe it's not even a bridge, maybe they just live on the same level.

Did you feel any connections with Fluxus?

I decided to become part of Fluxus in the 60s because I was probably the only person from the Eastern part of Europe who was working with media like happenings and events. They were very happy, all these people, Fluxus and so on, they were happy that somebody was there, and I was very happy they were there, because I was alone: there were no audiences in Prague for this kind of thing, they just looked at me like at a funny, crazy child... But it was beautiful to discover that there were people somewhere in the world who were close to me. I started friendships with George Maciunas, Allan Kaprow, Wolf Vostell. But I did not always agree with them, even if we were in the same boat; for me, Fluxus was conservative from the very beginning, because they always stayed on the stage. It was like they were always too much in art, and in the 60s I wanted to cross the border to social environments, social feelings, with everything, with music, with all my feelings. Therefore Fluxus was something I respect ed, but it was something like kindergarten, you know... I'm happy I was connected with Fluxus, because those people are brilliant, with strong ideas, and I'm always happy to meet them at exhibitions or concerts. But my work is a little different: I never did a small performance on the stage. In a way I'm much more conservative than Fluxus, because I just work with traditional media; on the other hand, I'm much more "avant-garde," because I left the field of art and went into real life, with the "happenings," for instance. Only a small part of my work really has to do with Fluxus.

(Paris, April 2, 1992)

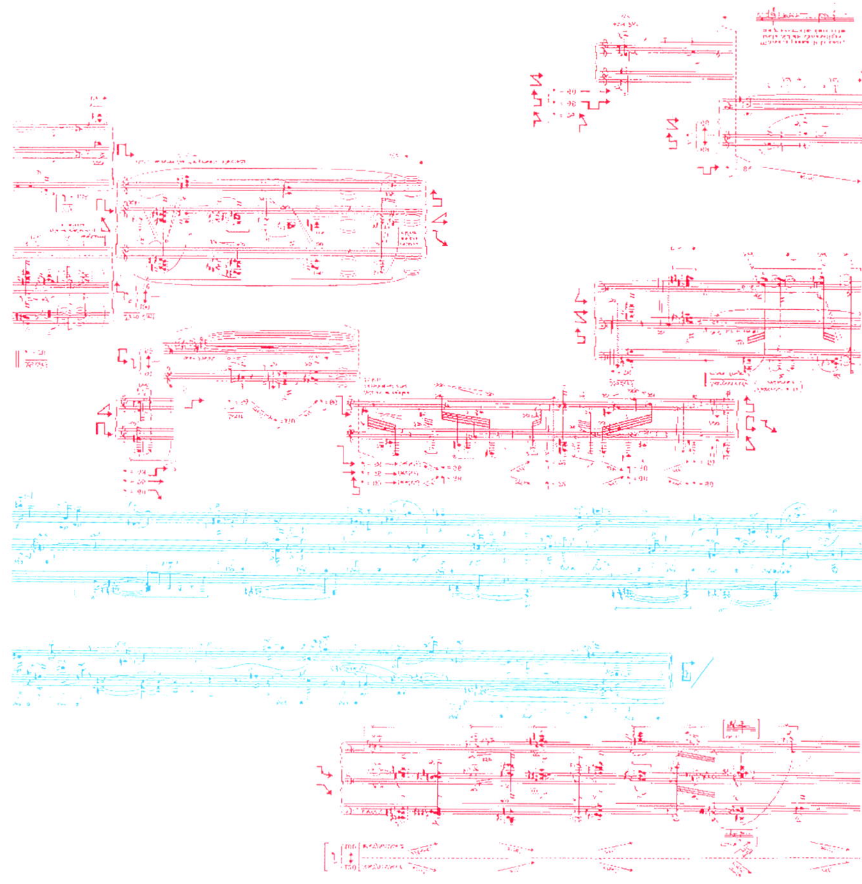

17 - Pierre Boulez,
Troisième sonate pour piano - *Formant 3 -Miroir*, **1957**
One page. (© Universal Editions)

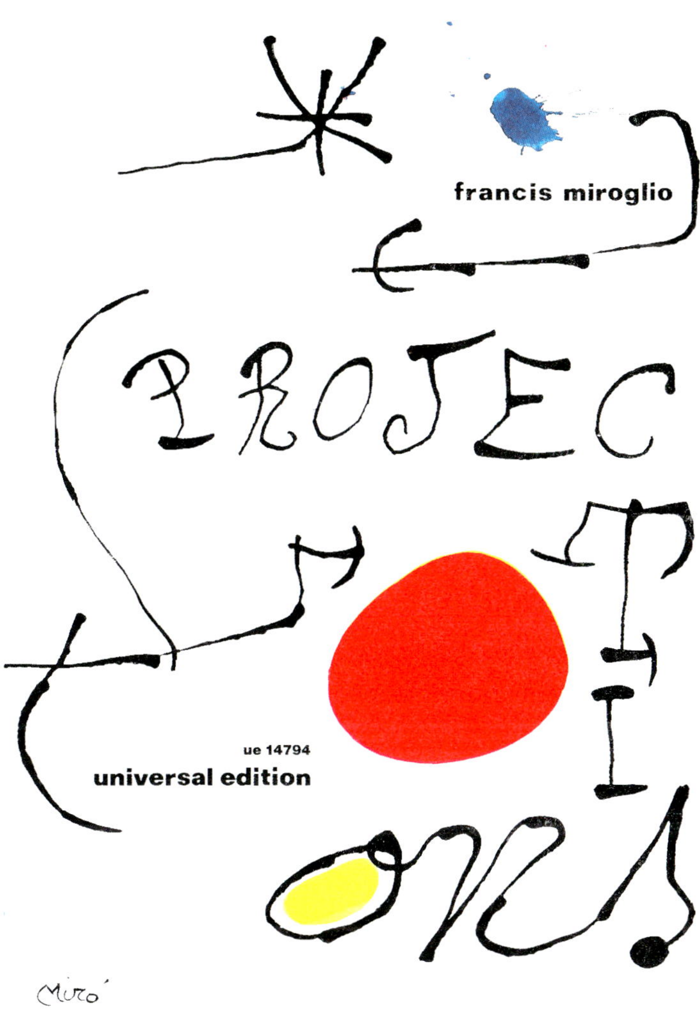

18 - Francis Miroglio, *Projections*, 1967
Front page of the musical score realized by Miró.
(© Universal Editions)

CHAPTER IV

Sound Sculptures

Assuming that work on notation makes it necessary to call upon a whole variety of possibilities for exchanges between music and the graphic arts, it goes without saying that recent sound objects have been constructed with both their plastic and musical qualities in mind from the very beginning. Such an aim has made it necessary for musicians to work in collaboration with architects and sculptors. Harry Partch (1901-1976) is considered as the founder of the "sound sculpture" movement, which aims to make the visual and acoustic qualities of invented instruments interact, and thus involve the whole personality of each individual, whether observer or participant, in a sort of acoustic magic, or in ritual experience. Partch, who judged European music to be "incorporeal," expected music to appeal to the eye, and not just the ear. In his opinion, music, words, dance, and the lute family of instruments had to fuse in a perfect unity of aesthetic intention.

From the 1940s onwards, the sculptor Harry Bertoia, whose approach is very closely related to the spiritual aims developed by Fischinger in California, produced over a hundred "sounding brasses," in bronze, beryllium or nickel, all assemblages of different sized tubes which could produce vibrations of both acoustic and visual dimensions. Since then, the "sound sculpture" movement has not ceased to expand. Bernard and François Baschet, speaking on the subject of their "sound structures," which have been presented in museums, and performed in concert and for studio recordings, claim the following: "We have tried to create a synthesis between sculpture and sound, because it seems clear to us that there exist firm links between sound and physical forms... The principle of these structures is to avoid using electricity or electronic devices, a principle which therefore remains true to historical instrumental tradition. The advantages of these "structures" over electronics may be felt when it comes to creating new sounds, [...] the performer is then in physical contact with the vibration. [...] The structures can also be employed to decorate the stage."

The scope of Baschet's instrumentation has become progressively more and more varied since the beginning of the 1950s. In particular, he has sought to fulfil pedagogical aims by putting together an ensemble of "structures." The problem arising implicitly from musical objects is that of their relation to the environment, which is why the Baschet brothers have, over the last few years, been working on "sound structures" intended for specific sites, which can be seen in the example of so-called musical fountains, which are perfectly integrated into open air places. Jacques Lasry has been working in conjunction with this research project since 1954.

The first acoustic sculptures by Jean Tinguely, *Mes étoiles – concert pour sept peintures (My Stars – Concert for Seven Paintings)*, date from 1958. Some of these works were the first in which he made use of percussion instruments. Switches placed on small panels enabled the audience itself to trigger off sound effects. At this time, while working on several projects in collaboration with Yves Klein, Tinguely seemed to be dematerializing the work of art somewhat, by resorting to acoustic sources which were partially invisible and ephemeral. The use of smoke, lights, smells, balls, explosives... confirms the existence of his desire to extend the range of sculpture beyond durable materials. In 1960, he organized a *Homage to New York* for the Museum of Modern Art, a piece which included a machine which destroyed itself. Ten arms, extending from old vehicles, were made to strike the keys of a piano. At the same time, this instrument was attached to an arrangement of cogwheels which also served to sound the notes.

The next phase of Tinguely's work followed in 1961 with his "radiophonic sculptures." Once Tinguely had thus established himself in the domain of sound, the composer Toshi Ichiyanagi was prompted to create a piece on the basis of sounds produced by his sculptures, which appeared in the catalogue (accompanied with a record) of a Tinguely exhibition in Tokyo, 1963. Musicians and poets took part in Tinguely's projects on several occasions. In 1970, for example, he preceded *Vittoria*—an event which took place in Milan on the occasion of the tenth anniversary of the Nouveau Réalisme movement—with a vocal performance by François Dufrêne. Later on, many of Tinguely's projects included processions, or parades, in which sound played an important role. In this way, the artistic event was tending to become a sort of carnival or masquerade.

The *Méta-harmonies* date from 1985 and testify in particular to Tinguely's close attention to the relation between machines and sound. Here, the sounds specific to the various movements of machines are complemented by the sounds of musical instruments like pianos, cymbals, drums, and wood-blocks... *Fata Morgana*, which is incorporated into the *Méta-harmonies,* proves to be a genuine sound factory. "I manage to disturb everything by means of sounds which move about. Two or three of the percussion instruments are linked together, but you would have to wait for years in order to hear the same sequence of sound twice," claimed Tinguely. This work therefore made it possible to introduce a degree of disorder at the heart of the source of acoustic material, which thus opened up the composition to elements of chance and unpredictability.

In the work of Takis, the treatment of sound often seems to be inseparable from those projects he bases on plastic environments. In 1963, he created his first musical sculptures in the form of magnetic pendulums, consisting of a large needle suspended such that it could strike a piano string, and a ball and block of cork containing magnetized metal inside them. The objects made of cork were intended to bump into each other when vibrating, then to give a muffled stroke to the block.

During the same year, he produced a cathodic arrangement called *Bruit du vide (Sound of Emptiness)*, "tuned" by Earle Brown, and which serves as an illustration of the idea of objects or instruments employed as *receivers,* rather than sources of sound. Physical and mechanical properties alone make up the "score," which plays continuously once the process is set in motion. From 1965 onwards, he used sculptures, electromagnets, and pendulums in close conjunction by organizing them into electromagnetic musical environments. The materials chosen to be struck by hammers equipped with electromagnets and switches hung from the ceiling were usually either types of gongs consisting of steel sheets, or ready-made objects collected by the artist himself. However, Takis considered the gongs to be too "musical," and quickly took steps to alter the conception and construction of the materials needed for his environments by selecting or gauging them according to the space in which the sound sculptures were to take effect. This is how, from 1974 onwards, he came to organize what became known as "musical spaces."

1979 was the year in which Takis composed his "electro-musicals," presented in the form of scenes. For each object, a steel needle strikes a string stretched across the surface of the canvas, the sound produced being amplified electronically. Whenever a number of Takis' "musicals" take place together in one exhibition room, they produce an aleatory combination of sounds, lending genuinely acoustic qualities to space which enable the listener to experience a constantly changing environment, in spite of the fixed nature of each object. Takis therefore sets up an extremely controlled device, which nevertheless permits sound phenomena to interact in unpredictable ways, in infinitely varying constellations.

The notion of participation, when applied to some of Takis' sound sculptures, takes on a completely different meaning from that normally associated with public events. In order to avoid acoustic experience remaining available only to people who already have a command of instrumental technique, some musicians and plasticians advocate using the widest possible variety of sound sources or objects. Hugh Davies, for example, accompanies exhibitions involving sound ateliers with a display of what might be called score-objects, designed for "instruments" generally made out of common consumer objects. Davies does not compose with a particular instrument in mind, but constructs his own instrument according to the sound material he seeks to render. He uses either objects he finds by chance, like the microphones in the piece *Telephone-Bell-Tree,* the encyclopaedias with their pages torn out and turned into instruments, as in *Squeakbox,*—or everyday objects which he puts to a new, inhabitual use, like the kitchen utensils in *Culinary Shozyg.* Davies therefore brings into focus arrangements and constructions which vary according to their context, whether this involves an exhibition, concert, or multimedia event...

Among the artists who have devoted part of their activities to what is generally known as "sound sculpture," one could mention Pol Bury, John Appleton, Max Eastley, Joe Jones, Paul Panhuysen, and Terry Fox.

Takis

To start with, I wasn't intending to contruct "musicals," but sought to create a magnetic musical piece, which I call a "symmetrical figure," by using a string and metallic sphere which could move up and down. In actual fact, I created my first "musical" as a result of me reaching a little higher than usual and taking hold of the sphere. When I did this, the electric current was cut off, the sphere fell on to the string, and the object thus acquired an acoustic dimension. I was very impressed by this, because I had always dreamt of being a musician. From this moment on, I took to constructing all sorts of other instruments, which were shown either in exhibitions or during performances, in particular with Nam June Paik, Charlemagne Palestine and Joelle Léandre. These people were professional musicians, and therefore always used instruments set up specifically in exhibition spaces, whereas I am a musician without really wanting to be one, and have received no musical education. However, we share the same conceptions about art, and see eye to eye, enjoying a sort of intellectual harmony.

Since 1964, I have been relying on intuitions for my work. Electromagnetism is not a field of research which lends itself to mathematical calculations, because it does not function according to linear laws, and its results are very difficult to evaluate. If you fix a string directly to a board, for example, the result is quite different than if the string is attached to the wall, and if a magnetic hammer strikes a tube, the sound is nothing like that produced by a wooden beam. In every case, I am looking for a specific result. I insist on the fact that this experimentation is a form of research, not a mere construction of gadgets and contraptions. I call my music "magnetic music," and the instruments used to make this, "musicals." They can be made of every possible type of material. The first one I made was of wood. This consisted of a plank a little like a door, with a taut string attached to two fixing points. An electromagnet was installed behind the door to make the string vibrate, which was struck by a metal rod situated in front of the door. This is how the instrument was presented to the public, without any additional explanations.

My "musicals" are not composed. Even if I plan out a lot of factors in advance while constructing a piece, I always leave room for chance. My role in the acoustic end product lies essentially in the choice of string, its length, and the degree of magnetic force used to strike the string. Once you set the instrument in motion, the instrument itself becomes its own agent, and acts of its own accord. This is therefore a "virtual" musical composition. If someone tells me I'm a musician, I end up by replying "Yes, perhaps I am?" I am a musician who constructs his own instruments. On the other hand, the instrument also transforms me into a musician.

You nevertheless remain interested in both visual and acoustic aspects of art?

Yes, I insist a lot on the visual aspect. A twelve-meter long beam, for example, is an extraordinary instrument. Providing I have done my sums properly, a beam like this would already suffice to give me a piece of music, as would a tube of twelve meters in length, and sixty centimeters in diameter. These gigantic proportions are very significant in my work. I am probably the only artist who works with such huge instruments, like the one I recently created out of the water tower at Beauvais, which was sixty-five meters high. Every installation of my "musicals" depends on the acoustics of the exhibition space put at my disposal. My work as a composer lies very much in knowing how to arrange the positions of each instrument, in what I call a "musical space." I have to test this space before finding adequate instruments to suit it, by trying out either tubes, or metallic strips, etc. All this is done intuitively.

Since your first "musicals," the interest in what is called "sound sculpture" has not stopped increasing. Do you feel any affinity for other "sound sculptors?"

I don't think the different sound sculptors can be compared. Several composers, including John Cage for example, have made it known (in a light-hearted manner, that is) that they are jealous of my instruments. Naturally, Tinguely has also made use of sound with his own kind of humor. I try to express something different, however, a kind of music *in* space, and not simply music inspired by a sound sculpture.

Do you aim to show how space itself can be musical?

Yes, I transform space into a musical phenomenon. In the case of the water tower at Beauvais, for example, I am convinced that the result was a form of cosmic sound. This sixty-five-meter high building, being attacked from all sides by wind eddies which set the strings vibrating, produced a real sort of cosmic variation. On hearing that, one feels at one with space.

There is occasionally an element of chance in what you do. It therefore seems that you do not exclude certain aleatory effects from your works, depending on the sites in which they take place.

Some aspects of my work are certainly not calculated, or organized rigidly in advance. My role is to determine the tension of the strings, what objects are to strike them, and the nature of the materials. However, I do not intervene a second time to adjust an installation of "musicals." For my installation at the Pompidou Center in 1990, for example, a number of changes occurred to the sound I had proposed at the beginning, over which I had no control. Once the sounds are created, space takes over to guide and shape the waves. The result varies according to the way in which the hammer strikes the string, the distances between the strings themselves, or the number of visitors in the exhibition room, all of which renders the overall sound more or less sharp, or flat, and determines the reverberation time...

You are therefore concerned with determining a sort of initial line of action, after which the sounds are left to take their own course...

Exactly. I don't aim to control all these variations, as a composer would. Apart from this, I very rarely return for a second time to the site of an installation. This reminds me too clearly of the nightmares I used to have before constructing the instruments. I see no reason why I should relive this feeling of terror. Once the work is over, I forget, I disappear.

(Paris, March 18, 1992)

CHAPTER V

Beyond artistic categories

At the beginning of the fifties, particularly in the United States, artistic practices evolved which left behind for good the goal of establishing cause and effect relations between the various modes of activity brought face to face. Each mode in question was granted a relative autonomy in its functioning, which could be more appropriately described in terms of an interpenetration, rather than a parallel comparison, of elements stemming from several different artistic fields.

In 1952 at the Black Mountain College, John Cage took the initiative of presenting a musical action considered as one of the antecedents of the "happening." Following a conference on Zen Buddhism, and a reading of texts by Master Eckhardt, he staged a version of *Imaginary Landscape n° 4* for radio sets. During the performance, Robert Rauschenberg put on old records, David Tudor played a prepared piano, while Merce Cunningham and several others danced down the aisles. White canvases by Rauschenberg had been hung on the walls.

It goes without saying that the result emanating from this kind of event is an interpenetration of disparate phenomena, in which the identity of each remains intact. No hierarchy whatsoever could be detected between the elements, both visual and sonorous, which were destined to meet only momentarily, in the space of a split second.

A similar effect occurred in a concert organized by J. Cage in 1961 in Paris, where the principal participants were David Tudor, Jasper Johns, Niki de Saint-Phalle, and Jean Tinguely... On this occasion, R.

Rauschenberg staged in public a "combine painting," equipped to produce sound by means of contact microphones.

The invention of the word "happening" seems to originate from the American artist Allan Kaprow. His first happenings date back to 1957 on the occasion of his environment-collages at George Segal's farm in New Jersey. According to Kaprow, a happening is an environment containing a temporal dimension which is integrated into a place having nothing to do with art, and which generally gives the impression of being a unique event. To paraphrase a remark by Kaprow, space and time become less pictorial and musical than topical, relevant to the present. The things propelled through space represent the very substance of sight, hearing, movement and individuals. Such immediacy should necessarily be evident in happenings, actions which, for J. Cage, "aren't like life, but should be able to be consumed in relation to our lives."

In 1959, *18 Happenings in 6 Parts* was staged. Apart from words painted on the walls, the visual aspect of this work consisted in a film and slide show. R. Rauschenberg and J. Johns each painted the two respective sides of a canvas. The acoustic aspect was provided by actions dispersed around the space of the gallery, which itself was divided into three rooms. The listener-spectators were issued with cards telling them when, how, and in what direction they were to move during the course of the happening.

Even if his approach was soon revealed to be a determining factor operating in favor of actions which relied on the shock effect of extremely heterogeneous occurrences, it was nonetheless precisely on this occasion in 1959 that J. Cage distanced himself from this kind of activity. He realized in particular that the protagonists of this event expected certain reactions from the public in advance. "Whenever I go to see a happening which seems to be governed by an intention of some kind, I start off by saying that it doesn't interest me. On top of that, I didn't like being told to move from one room to the other in *18 Happenings in 6 Parts.* For although I'm not engaged in politics, I do, as an artist, have certain intuitions about the political contents of art, and art doesn't contain the police.[1]" A. Kaprow subsequently gave up using the term "happening," because he found it too vague and so, from the beginning of the seventies onwards, preferred to use the term "activity."

J. Cage tends to allow a multiplicity of events, whether visual or auditory, to coexist and accumulate in processes like *Theater Piece* or *Variations,* immersing the listener-spectator in a situation whose outcome effectively depends on the choices of each individual. The actions and publications of the group Fluxus (literally, "that which flows"), founded in 1961 by George Maciunas, on the other hand, present us with the alternative of an extreme reduction, a miniaturization of the material presented to human perception. It is as if the aim of this group was to concentrate an action into a single event, in as concise a manner as possible. The majority of "events" staged by the Fluxus group, in particular those of George Brecht, can characteristically be identified as standing between several different modes of communication, between poetry, theatrical representation and musical production, between art and everyday life.

The group Fluxus, formed mainly in the United States and in Germany, never really gave voice to a manifesto. According to G. Brecht, who began as a painter, the individual members got together spontaneously to publish and carry out their work "with something inexpressible in common," which placed them on the fringes of what can be defined as art. Their actions derive, claims G. Maciunas, "from the monostructural and theatrical qualities of a simple natural event, of a game or a gag. They are a combination of Spike Jones, vaudeville, gags, children's games, and Duchamp."

Seen against the background of daily life, these events sometimes actually get mixed up and blend in with daily life itself. The extremely varied assortment of objects and toys goes to show that absolutely

(1) — John Cage, "La salive" ("Saliva"), in *Le théâtre 1968.1*, Editions Christian Bourgois, Paris, 1968.

anything can be substituted for art, that the confines of art are infinitely more extensible than might seem, so long as sight and hearing are linked together, and thoughts provoked. Most actions make their impression as jointly acoustic and visual phenomena. In this way, La Monte Young's *Fire Piece* should lead the audience to "listen to what one normally only sees, or vice versa."

G. Brecht claims that in his approach, the concept of "event" goes back to 1960. The idea dawned on him while he was waiting for his wife one evening next to his car, the motor running, with the left indicator flashing. He turned this into the first piece he made which included the word "event," *Motor Vehicle Sundown Event.* For him, the "event scores" are poetry which become "actions" via the intermediary of music.

Some of these events are not even intended to be presented in public, but destined to remain private, such as *3 Telephone Events* by George Brecht, in which each event represents a search for precise points of intersection with reality.

Certain events deliberately provoke a feeling of insecurity, as can be seen in *Danger Musics* by Dick Higgins. Open cynicism is often shown towards cultural values, in *Solo pour violin 62* by G. Maciunas for example, where the instrument is progressively mistreated, then destroyed. In *Pièces de public* by Ben, the public is subjected to aggression. In the duets by the cellist Charlotte Moorman and Nam June Paik, one can sense latent violence. Other works underline the sexuality inherent in instrumental play: Nam June Paik's *Opéra sextronique* thus laid claim to the sexual emancipation of musical practice. At its first performance in New York in 1967, Charlotte Moorman was arrested for indecency because she was playing bare-chested. Nam June Paik responded by denouncing the pre-Freudian hypocrisy of the musical avant-garde which remained, in spite of its so-called emancipation movements—serialism, indetermination, action music—closed in by the confines of its outmoded puritanism.

Over and above music and the plastic arts, the proposals put forward by the Fluxus group take on the characteristics of a philosophical investigation, independently of all criteria of aesthetic judgement, and tend more generally to claim the status of a veritable art of living. Actions by Fluxus possess a collective dimension which distinguishes them from the initiatives of its members in Germany for example, like those of Joseph Beuys and Wolf Vostell.

In the work of Beuys, the grand piano, symbol of the concert par excellence, becomes an instrument of silence, with its keyboard and lid firmly closed. Occasionally, the piano is even wrapped up in felt, or one of its pedals broken off. Freed from its material function, the instrument takes on an emblematic character, where its enigmatic quality plays an active role. Beuys never used the terms "happening," "event" or "performance," preferring that of "action" instead.

"The acoustic element and the sculptural quality of sound have always been essential for me in art. In terms of music, it is possible that my past with the violin and cello encouraged me in this direction. In addition, there was the use of sound as a sculptural material in order to widen the global understanding of sculpture from the point of view of how materials should be put to use. Consequently, everything becomes material for sculpture—not only solid materials like metal, clay, and stone, but also sound, noises, or a melody based on language—and all of these things acquire their form through thought. Thought is therefore adopted as a tool for sculpture. This is, of course, an extreme position to take, the truly transcendental position for production in general."

More generally, Beuys' project is situated at the meeting point of several different levels of language, mixing up linguistic signs, sounds, notations. The *Symphonie sibérique,* from 1963 was his first Fluxus action in Düsseldorf. This began with a piano solo, then a piece by Satie, during which Beuys hung a dead hare on a blackboard. Next, small heaps of clay, with branches planted in them, were placed on the piano. A steel wire serving as a conductor connected the piano to the hare. During the action, Beuys extracted the hare's heart. According to him, this was by no means the reflection of a post-Dadaist attitude. "I want to express a meaningful relation containing lots of material concerning birth and death. The conversion into matter, as carried out on the hare, appears here for the first time in reality during this concert. This has got nothing to do with those neo-Dada actions designed to scare the bourgeois." In fact, the materials he uses are there in order to reveal their energetic value.

"It is generally agreed that writing is an expression of language. But language is also an image, and language is original. Music is also a description of something. We must not forget that there are many possibilities available for expression. Scores by Beethoven or Mozart, or any other composer, are also images, physical expressions. Without this physical dimension, nothing would be possible [...]. Mankind has most probably *said* something with the images it has created, and, likewise, most attempts at articulating ideas with language can certainly be interpreted musically.[2]"

"Fluxus is like a collective (like a kolkhoz) and not something which resembles a second self. In this respect, Fluxus is distinct from your dé-coll/age," wrote Maciunas to Wolf Vostell in 1964. For W. Vostell, "everything is plastic music, that is visual, because the acoustics are tied up with different time processes, whereas the artificial composition of music is produced differently each time, though with the same instruments. Since 1958, I have used the term "dé-coll/age music" for those acoustic processes which result from chance de-composition: an electric light bulb is smashed, posters are torn down, and this shock is relayed through the amplifier. From that moment on, the shock of falling objects, shouts of human beings in danger, sounds of car accidents, the background noise of a television, the fading of a radio, the multifarious noises made by the body etc., became my contribution to Fluxus music in Wiesbaden from 1962 onwards."

Interpenetration and open complexity seemed to become the domi-

(2) — Beuys' reply to Kounellis, in *Bâtissons une cathédrale,* Editions de l'Arche, Paris, 1988, pp.147-149; originally in *Ein Gespräch,* Parkett-Verlag, Zürich, 1986.

nant characteristics of the actions of artists like Robert Rauschenberg, Claes Oldenburg, Allan Kaprow or Ann Halprin, who choose polyvalent modes of activity, leading the painter to work with time, and the musician to compose with space. It is in this vein that R. Rauschenberg wrote several pieces, between 1963 and 1966, like *Pelican, Linoleum, Open Score,* all of which were accessible and open to the personal initiatives of the participants. "Art appears to me to be the residue of something which took place in the past... What interests me is being active, occupied. Everything I have done had only one aim, which is to see what would have happened if I had done one thing rather than another.[3]" However, this complexity, once operative, is not necessarily premeditated by the author. In the same way as when you walk in the streets, you may see people moving about with firm intentions, while at the same time being unaware of what their actual intentions are, so the artist may be aware of intentions, but not their content. Rather than analyzing in advance the elements of a planned situation, it soon became more and more appropriate to live reality in all its fundamentally experimental content, to somehow detach oneself from artistic illusion and, rather than playing a role, fully accept the identity of reality by paying as close attention as possible to the physical properties of what is offered to be seen and heard in the present.

The same situation applies to some of the assemblages by R. Rauschenberg, in particular *Oracle* (1965), which combined a bathtub with a shower, a length of piping mounted on iron wheels, a staircase on castors, the upright of a window, and a car door, all of these elements including a battery, a receiving set and a loudspeaker. The receivers swept along the waveband of the New York radio stations. A motor, remote controlled by a member of the audience, scanned the radio from one wavelength to another at varying speeds, as if it were picking up the sonorous messages of an entire city. For R. Rauschenberg, *Oracle* represents the successful outcome of his research on sound collages, destined to act contrapuntally with visual collages.

(3) — R. Rauschenberg quoted by R. Kostelanetz, in *The Theatre of Mixed Means,* The Dial Press, New York, 1968, pp.78-79.

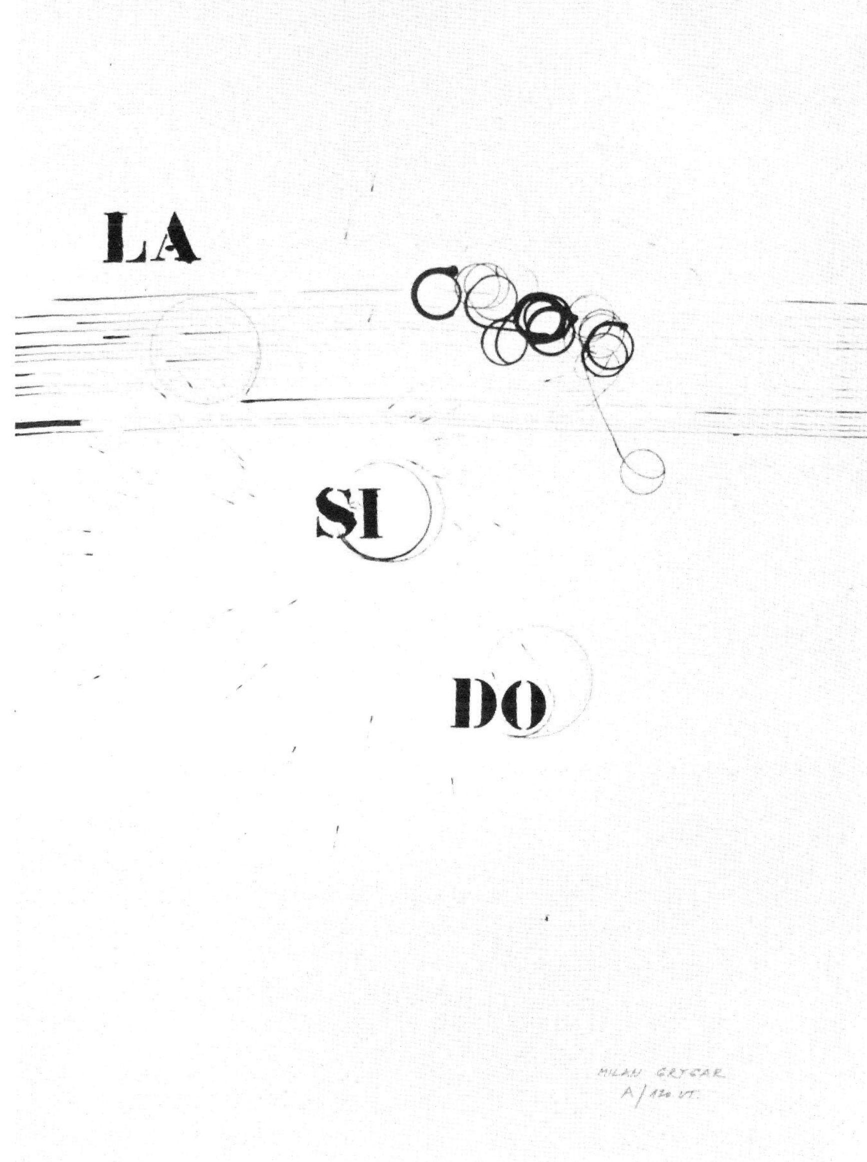

19 - Milan Grygar, ***LA, SI, DO*****, 1966**
Acoustic drawing (88 x 62,5 cm - Indian ink on paper)
photo by Stefan Grygar (collection of the artist)

This breakaway from traditional artistic categories can also be found in the productions of the group Zaj, created in Spain by Juan Hidalgo in collaboration with Walter Marchetti and Esther Ferrer, or in book-scores like *Seven Miniatures* by Tom Phillips, certain scores by the Scratch Orchestra, *Mo-no, Musik zum lesen* by Dieter Schnebel, or in *Teatrino* by Giuseppe Chiari.

The fields of lettrisme (Isidore Isou, Maurice Lemaître...), of sound poetry, visual or concrete poetry (Bernard Heidsieck, Henri Chopin, François Dufrêne, Brion Gysin or Gerhard Rühm) themselves stand in-between established categories. Depending on which process was implemented, these artists were led to resort to the most appropriate means of expression and use, in turn, supports such as magnetic tape, the space of graphic works or books, or even explore the possibilities of the human voice and body through performance. The oeuvre of each of these artists proves to what extent the persistence of divisions between different artistic practices has become outdated nowadays. The material they explore, signs, phonemes, letters etc., inevitably leads them to take on a polyvalent activity, which occasionally slips imperceptibly from one artistic field to another.

In Milan Grygar's work, it is remarkable how the transition from sound to silence via drawings occurs in a completely organic way. In one type of drawing, which he calls an "acoustic drawing," the tools destined to mark dots and lines on the page—including several mechanical toys which partially escape his control—produce percussive sonorous events, in which the different elements making up this acoustic environment follow their own course, like many instruments simultaneously playing different pieces, while leaving visible traces as they pass. M. Grygar was therefore able to choose between several different ways of proceeding with such an activity. Either he exposed the drawing to the public at the very moment of its production, which was both sonorous and visual, in the form of an action (either live, or pre-recorded on video), or he exhibited the drawing later on, in a state of silence and immobility. Alternatively, he played the recording made on the spot during the graphic action and presented this as a sound event in its own right, or else he presented the drawing to musicians so that they could use it as a basis for experimenting on new hypotheses for play.

As a result of the advent of new kinds of technology in this field of artistic interactions, the possibilities for dialogue between various practices were invariably encouraged to branch out and extend in scope. Even if the task of putting them into practice did not rely on sophisticated technical devices, interactive projects served to contribute a great deal to opening the way for the multimedia events which were to grow in number from the seventies onwards.

Wolf Vostell

In 1954, when I discovered the principle of "dé-coll/age," which consists in breaking down forms and categories, both concrete and invisible, I noticed that all alterations of form produced noises. The same goes for biochemical processes in the brain. "What sounds do cerebral currents produce at the precise moment they are engaged in musical thought?" Take my piece *Kleenex*, for example. When the light bulb is smashed, it no longer produces light, but sound. A car accident produces its own acoustics, when the price to pay for this can even lead to fatal consequences. This music from real life was my contribution to Fluxus in 1962. The ambivalence of our lives produces inexplicable events. Ritual life is accompanied by sounds. Life as sound, sound as life. In the second half of the twentieth century, it is more satisfying and more important, from a socio-aesthetic point of view, to listen to two jet engines for the duration of a four-hour air flight than to spend four hours sat immobile listening to an opera by Wagner. My conception of multimedia consists in juxtaposing existing acoustic processes, and mixing them with body actions: life is art, and art is life. Since 1959, I have been writing scores of my happenings, or of action music, in the form of hand-written notes or telegraphic-style instructions. Try, for example, catching a bus on the PC line ("petite ceinture," inner beltway skirting the periphery of Paris), and during the whole four-hour journey, do nothing except listen very closely to all the things contributing to the sounds round about.

Since the seventies, I have been subjecting scores by Mozart, Scarlatti and Bach to "dé-coll/age." I like music which advances slowly like a tortoise. I also like repetitions which operate tautologically, along with rituals or actions involving the human body, all models representing forms of life. Destruction, night-time, and irony are all types of musical material. Of course, when paper is torn up, a tremendous noise is produced. The form and duration of this noise can be energized, by tearing more quickly, or more slowly, almost like a simple instrument. Moreover, later on in Cologne in 1961, one of the Fluxus composers, Benjamin Peterson, wrote a homage in my honor, a "paper-décollage," for the preview of an exhibition of my dé-coll/ages. He composed a tearing up of different kinds of paper, while playing on the amplification of the tones associated with the act of tearing.

As far as my own work is concerned, I successfully realized several Fluxus compositions according to the principles of décollage, tearing up posters, and erasing marks from a page, which appears in my oeuvre after the "dé-coll/age" period. The action of erasing can be amplified by means of a microphone, which I often did before an audience. The microphone is held manually, and the erasing, carried out with a piece of cloth rubbed on the paper, has an effect quite unlike that of tearing. In the piece *Kleenex* (1962), the action consisted in smashing a hundred light bulbs on the ground. Originally, the noise was not amplified, because we did not really give much thought to the use of microphones at that time. Later on, I sometimes did make use of microphones, which rendered the sound much more plastic. The effect of acoustic magnification by means of microphones is really something quite delightful, very impressive...

When I was a student in Paris, I heard a record of concrete music by the group of Pierre Schaeffer and Pierre Henry. They recorded sounds from the environment, then distorted them. However, distorting sounds in the studio subsequent to their production did not interest me. I was concerned with the phenomenological sounds of a piece, but not as a form of material only to be worked over after the sound event proper. This is what distinguishes my approach from that of concrete music and synthetic music, as practiced by K. Stockhausen on the basis of electronically generated material.

In your opinion, therefore, tearing up, or erasing, are acts with both acoustic and visual impact...

Absolutely. And I don't mean acoustic in the sense of before or after the event, but the acoustic phenomenon itself, of one particular action as it is produced live. This is why the term "music-action" is perfectly justifiable.

When you stage actions, do you aim to draw the listener into the scene itself, to induce him or her to perceive simultaneously the event and its representation?

No, the aim is to make the listener more sensitive, to make his perception more phenomenological. It must be born in mind that I set up many environments with a very strong acoustic element. This is a prime case of audience participation, for in an environment, things can be carried out in accordance with the environment, where one is free to behave differently than in real life. In this case, there aren't only visual phenomena and the music of noises, but also the climate, and the sensibility of listeners. It may suffice, as an example of what I mean, to walk through a puddle of water... The executant, the "performer," should then feel capable of listening to the sounds he himself produces, as well as those defined in the environment by the artist. Early on, for my happening in Ulm, for example, which I judge to be one of my best acoustic pieces, there was a very simple scene. It took place in a monastery, where we arrived at dusk, about three hundred of us, in five buses. The action consisted simply in each "performer," armed with a chunk of wood picked up in the courtyard of the monastery, walking in single file around the inside of the courtyard, which was very wide. Everyone simply had to strike the wall with the piece of wood... the action involved nothing more than walking and striking the wall. Three hundred people each striking in a different manner, this created a fantastic effect. This was back in 1964.

There are lots of acoustic ideas involved in happenings, but nobody has really investigated the various musical aesthetics of Fluxus, even though every artist from Fluxus has his own personal aesthetic ideas. I for my part have realized about fifty-three proper happenings in my lifetime, and nearly all of them include some acoustic participation. This remains, however, an aspect of our research which is not mentioned in any catalogue, or on any record.

Do you treat sound in the same way as the other materials you use, or do you have a different approach specific to the field of sound?

Personally, I cannot live without sound or music. I have thought a lot about my situation, and have come to the conclusion that if I don't listen to composed sounds, I fall sick! During the whole of the time I work in the studio, I always listen to lots of music, often music which is contrary in nature to what I am doing. If I am constructing an object which is melancholy in nature, or critical towards my experiences at that moment, I choose baroque music, because I don't want the music to be an illustration of my feelings. I thus escape from the age we live in and draw strength from baroque music to help me along. In any case, I have the impression that the drawing I'm working on ought at least have the force of a piece by Handel or of some other composer from that time. I have a very good ear, and it's a pleasure for me to be on the highway or in an airport, where I register every tiny variation of sound, the result being that I'm accompanied by pleasant acoustic sensations during every moment of my life. Unlike a lot of people, for me, these sounds are not a nightmare.

Are there some contemporary composers who have interested you in particular, or who seem to be party to your approach?

Karlheinz Stockhausen. He is one of the first people I visited, which was in 1954, in his studio in Cologne. He was very proud to be able to create everything with computers, electronically generated material etc., and I liked the sounds he made. In fact, I still like K. Stockhausen's electronic music, but the end product depends a lot on the engineer with whom he is working, i.e. if a different composer works with the same engineer, the results are more or less identical. This was the case for Mauricio Kagel and Nam June Paik in Cologne. Neither of them could really create anything in the Cologne studio at that time, because it was really part of Stockhausen's project, with his own engineer. With the increase in technical means of production, it's technology which begins to dictate style.

Whereas you yourself seek to bring under control single-handedly the sonorous result of those "actions" containing an acoustic element?

Yes. An example of this is a work of mine called *Bêcher,* exhibited in Cologne. It consists of a big box with earth inside. In the earth there are cables, which are connected to loudspeakers. The audience is invited to dig over (in French, "bêcher") the earth with a spade. When the cables are touched, and depending on how they are touched, they produce all sorts of rumblings, as if a thunderstorm were taking place in the room. If the cables are not touched during the digging, *Bêcher* remains a mere box full of earth.

These works are therefore installations which you devise yourself, in collaboration with engineers.

Yes, I tell the engineer what type of sounds I require, and he produces them. Every single technical process is unique in kind, thought up for a specific project.

Apart from Mauricio Kagel, who you worked with on the film Duo, *are there any other composers with whom you have started up a sort of collaboration or exchange?*

Very early on, I felt an affinity for Pierre Henry in Paris. But he too was a studio musician, unlike myself, for I only work in a studio when I want to rehearse a sound, for example. Mixing one sound with another, as practiced in concrete music, doesn't interest me. I have a weakness for sounds which are pure, not modulated.

Do you have a partiality for one sound universe in particular? You said that, while working, you like to listen to certain kinds of music opposed to what you are doing, but these types of music do not occur in your actions. Here, on the contrary, quite different sounds can be heard.

That's true, but I have no prejudices against any one form of music, with a few exceptions, Wagner, for instance, or excessively heavy composers like that, or perhaps even Italian opera from the 19th century. Otherwise, I like almost all forms of music. I frequently spend time in Spain, and Radio Nacional 2 broadcasts classical music all day long, so I leave the radio on all the time. In fact, I have a strong desire to learn and listen to musical forms from the past, in all their diversity. This represents an inexhaustible, rich source of inspiration for me, which I'm similarly aware of when I look at trees... a sort of environment, which may not seem very important while I am working on my art, but which enables me to be immersed in a sonorous atmosphere of considerable wealth. Moreover, as far as I am concerned, a car provides a musical object in its own right. Occasionally, though I don't know why, the motor of my car sounds different, and I notice the changes taking place. It is possible to notice the sound, the noises of each individual part, the doors, and so on... This is how I came to create a certain number of small-scale pieces, for example *Musique-Chambre*. This dates from the seventies, and involves opening and closing a car door seven hundred and fifty times. This piece can be performed by anyone, alone, in the countryside or in town, and remain a purely private experience. It can also be executed before an audience, which I did with four other people, the result being a superimposition of sounds and rhythms. The effect naturally becomes more complex still with a hundred people, and a hundred cars...

Wouldn't you say there is one type of sound in an environment which you seek out above all, a specific material?

No. Although a car door is one example of a specific material, after all.

Therefore, this can be a drinking glass at one moment, and a door at another... How should the events you organize be described: as "performances," happenings," "actions"?

The idea remains the same, but the usage is different in each case. In a chosen environment, or in a closed space, the acoustics are less readily available than in happenings, like those I am working on at the moment. The hundred four-door cars mingle in with the environment. If I seek to set up a more plastic, visual type of communication, I organize it in a big garage with an audience. If, on the other hand, I want the piece to unfold in a snowbound wood close by an airport, I go ahead and arrange to have these supplementary elements, the snow and the airport, at my disposal. Towards the end of the fifties, it was evident that the boundaries between the different arts had been broken down. Painters began using time. Naturally, when a painter begins to use time, he automatically comes into contact with sound and composition.

The awareness of the element of time seems, in your experience, to coincide with a profound change in artistic notions. This transformation took place in your work at the end of the fifties...

That's true, I was conscious of this as from 1958, at the same time as the first really well organized Dada exhibition was mounted in October of the same year, in Düsseldorf. This spurred us all on, and we concluded that the idea of multimedia already existed in the work of Schwitters and the German Dadaists. We discovered the avant-garde movements in Russia, and the concert by Tatlin... and later on, of course, futurist music, Russolo's noise-producing instruments, which were different again from Dada, or concrete or electronic music, because they consisted in invented sounds, not sounds taken from everyday life. In short, it was a composition from life which gave rise to these sounds.

But you distinguished yourself very quickly in order to create your own project...

Yes, for even if I consider J. Cage, to cite one example, as being very inspired when he integrates noises which drift in through the door or the window, after a while I find that this can become tedious. Conceptually, it's excellent, even philosophical, but if you sit for ten years without a single noise reaching your ears, this risks becoming tiresome sooner or later. I am not an artist who always paints the same thing, but one who seeks variety. This is why I believe concepts are very important, but concepts alone, in the long run, do not fulfil ideas. This is why it is necessary to compose.

In fact, you smuggle in a certain number of deliberate intentions...

The impact of two cars amplified by microphones and loudspeakers constitutes the concept, and conveys meaning. To turn this into a message, however, it's necessary to take a hundred cars crashing together. The acoustic wealth is then greater, and the socio-psychological context more defined, because people are inevitably led to ask themselves precisely why a hundred cars crash into each other at the same time, in front of an audience.

So you have a precise result in mind...

Yes, but the result cannot be imagined in advance very precisely, because it's impossible to carry out rehearsals of such actions. That is why happenings are closely connected to life. If the concept is well thought out, the acoustic result will, whatever happens, be interesting from a phenomenological point of view, even if it cannot be weighed up in advance.

It is possible to envisage some of these actions or happenings being taken up by other artists, as if they were part of a score...

This is possible, but only if they are as rigorous as myself. A producer has no right to take the ideas and make the whole thing more pleasant, which would actually boil down to pure theater. There is a risk of misappropriating the idea of a happening by transforming it into entertainment.

What is your position as far as Fluxus artists are concerned?

My idea was not to specialize in certain materials. George Brecht specialized in minimal objects and processes, which is interesting, phenomenonologically speaking. I really like Dick Higgins' "visual music," Nam June Paik's "music-actions," as well as the early work of La Monte Young, especially his silent music, for example the piece which consists in feeding hay to a piano.

My contribution to Fluxus was made with the idea of "dé-coll/age," in other words, processes of decomposition conceived in the form of a sound idea. I concentrate on all the noises which are propagated when a form is destroyed. Other Fluxus artists use fixed forms. For example, in the famous work by G. Brecht, *Dripping Music,* the water keeps its original form, and the glass into which he throws the water remains the same. The difference with me is that I break the glass.

Your oeuvre is extremely complex, consisting of pictorial, fixed works, as well as mutable processes... How do the two coexist? I'm thinking in particular of Cri*:* Cri *is an event which took place two years ago, and is linked to plastic works which exist partially in the form of collages, etc. What bearing does the series of graphic works have on the event which has taken place, in your opinion?*

This is a very important question, which requires us to take a look at scores of happenings from the sixties. It is a form of experience which I myself have to come to terms with before executing the work. I take this precaution for the production of the work simply because I visualize it in my own mind beforehand, either in a dynamic form, or in the form of a material, or "objet trouvé." This choice changes as time goes on. In any case, I have to carry out a study of all these things in advance. For example, the six scores I made for the happening in Ulm thus make up a musical geography hour by hour—I can't find my bearings unless I have the movements of the actions on paper, and can see an hour's worth of movements on the page in front of me. It's too difficult to remember all that by heart. If, however, I see a drawing in note form, I at once remember the ideas represented by the marks or the words. The score functions as a notebook.

Are you interested in musical symbolics?

In *Cri,* a certain analogy can be discerned in the score. An example of this was provided on the occasion I found a broken jumbo jet, and associated it with the death of Ceaucescu, these being two forms of death, two things which disappear. Of course, subsequently, in *Cri,* I mention neither Ceaucescu nor the jumbo jet, but in acoustic terms, I choose, at this precise moment, to employ forty vacuum cleaners with maximum dynamics, along with the trombones. This is the high point of the concert.

Each element stands in relation to the other: the choice of sound material and those phenomena you combined by means of collage.

I transmit the force of the visual aspect into the domain of sound. In another "picture," where the dynamics are weak, the music also becomes weaker.

In one of the graphic plates of Cri, *you have inserted a preexisting score.*

Yes, in *Cri,* some pages of the Mozart quartets are "dé-coll/aged." The instrumentalist simply plays the notes he sees before him, which creates a kind of music resembling the style of Webern, consisting of four torn up scores, individual scores, and sub-scores destined for the instrumentalists. To be honest, I'm not able to present the whole score on one panel, for it would be huge. In the "notebook score," I find written down in black and white the principle elements I have to pay attention to when carrying out the project, but there are also sub-scores and lots of individual notes.

Have you worked on torn up scores for other projects?

I worked on fragments of a score by Bach for a concert in Madrid, and on one by Scarlatti for a Fluxus concert...

Do you then select one particular composer, or do you take any score at random, before tearing it up?

I tend to select a score I know, because I respect the music I tear up and transform, and because I can imagine the end result in advance.

Mesostic re Marcel Duchamp
(from M)

let Me
hAve
youR baggage;
i will Carry it for you.
no nEed:
i am wearing aLL of it.

20 - **John Cage**, *Mesostic*, 1980
(private collection)

But when you tear up the page of a score, you don't know exactly how the paper will behave...

That's true, it's a gestural act.

So, come what may, there is an element of chance, as well as an element of control... Do you play on the symbolic aspect, of either musical notation or of the means of communication which musicians develop among themselves?

No, this completely escapes me. The same thing occurs when you create a picture: nothing whatsoever matters any more, except the material. You have the paintbrush in one hand, and a tube of color in the other. There is no symbolism, no time for that. I don't even think of smoking any more. The act alone counts.

You are "tuned in" to the material.

Yes, in to the purity of elements.

So you have no preconceived ideas about the material you intend to use.

No, I take advantage of the possibilities offered by the materials. Only then does the artist come into his element. I don't want to work with materials that aren't natural.

Does everything fall into place at the same time when you create a project, that's to say the type of site, the type of sound, the type of environment?

Of course.

Take Fandango, *for example, this is a graphic work, but one which can just as well be played musically.*

Yes. Originally, it was a score by Bach, a gigue for violin. The violinist plays the notes he sees from left to right. All the black notes indicate silence, which means that there remains very little music on the two pages of notes. If you imagine the second violin faced with other deletions of notes, this results in a very strange polyphonic effect.

There are different types of perception involved when approaching a work like this. It can either be seen, or played... Do you give priority to one of these aspects, or do you consider them on equal terms?

During the concert, I give priority to the action, the acoustic end product.

Afterwards, however, this is a work which can be shown in an exhibition... Does silence play an important role for you?

Yes, of course, absolutely. It's always a game to see if silence exists or not. In fact, silence cannot exist, because the world is constantly moving, and the phenomena of nature are far from silent. It's the definition of silence which is interesting.

Sure, but by looking at Fandango *or the graphic plates in* Cri, *it is apparent that this is a score which can be read inwardly, as if it were the silent state of something which has the potential of turning into sound. Does this aspect interest you? In other words, do you think your graphic oeuvre can be first perceived in silence, only to be turned into something acoustic later on? A sort of dialectic of sound and silence...*

It's possible. But I myself am just as silent when faced with the drawing. Sound, that is, comes into my head at the very moment I am working on a piece. The process unfolds as follows: the outside world is virulent, whereas I am silent, so I effectively transform my acoustic sensations into drawings.

Nevertheless, there is some sound as you are working... When you carry out the principle of "dé-coll/age," you produce sound. Is this absorbed into the silence?

I think this is always the case. Sound is only emitted when action takes place. Without action, there exists merely the music of everyday life.

(Berlin, May 17, 1992)

Milan Grygar (interview conducted by Alexandre Broniarski)

Why did you distance yourself from painting in the early sixties?

I belonged to a generation whose former years had been spent looking at the work of Picasso, and which had been won over to the idea that painting was dead. When I gave up painting completely, my friends couldn't understand why. How could I, who was in love with color, give that up? Instead, drawing then seemed to me to be the only feasible way ahead for experimentation. I had already begun work at that time by exploiting the effects of chance, with Indian ink and paper dampened to improve its capillarity. For the most part, I produced drawings made of horizontal lines. From today's perspective, it is as if they were a prefiguration of my linear scores... One day, I picked up a piece of wood, and put it to work. My memory of this remains crisp clear, as something sudden, with silence and noise, the hammering of the page, the experience of sound. I started work again with a tape recorder. I played, rewound the tape, listened to it again, and understood. From that moment on, I had discovered what was to affect me even more than color, which was sound, the acoustic event.

The different peoples of your country take pride in a rich musical heritage. Wasn't your development therefore in some way predetermined by this?

Yes. I was raised with the sound of music in my ears. We were all living near to the border with Hungary, in South Slovakia. I was born in Zwollen. I can remember that time as clearly as if it were yesterday, how I was enraptured while listening to wind instruments, or to the gypsies and their children playing by intuition. Their skill fascinated me to the point where I became intoxicated. Later on, at the Academy, I learnt to play the violin. I think I must have been permanently marked by the feeling of extreme precision instilled in me by the virtuosos. Every one of my drawings, and every performance aspires to this perfection. Chance plays a role as well, of course, though in a similar way to beauty, invariably unforseeable and constantly dazzling.

How did you embody in concrete terms the connections between plastic events and acoustic events?

The first acoustic drawings were carried out with only one hand, as I painted by using only my right hand and one single instrument. I chose objects which were familiar to me, all very ordinary: a piece of wood to start with, followed by a tin box, then a metal comb, a fine tool used for collecting blueberries. There was also a hand bell, though not for drawing with, but for the benefit of its timbre, which left an invisible trace of sound. I wanted to superimpose sounds on one another, to create something like the polyphonic effect I like so much in pre-classical music. It was under the guidance of this intuitive idea that I began to use clock components. I inked the axes, set them in motion, and they pivoted of their own accord, prolonging one after the other the impulses of my hand with a similar effect to a humming top, or a gyroscope, which ultimately fell out of equilibrium. The whole thing happened very quickly. The toothed cogs whirled around, their axes tracing circles, rotating on an ever wider circumference. At the high point of its motion, it topples over, circles around once more, and comes to rest, leaving nothing but immobility and silence, upon which the drawing is complete. I note down the time elapsed, and also the space taken up by the sequence on the magnetic tape.

What is an acoustic drawing? Could you define it?

The silence of my studio helped me to overcome the silence of drawing itself. I could hear all the sounds coming from outside, birdsong, children's shouting, the banging noise made by a woman beating a carpet in the courtyard. One day, I suddenly noticed the sounds of my own rhythms. Acoustic drawings could be described as a new plastic experience, aided by music—or rather the graduation of sound and its reverberation—and as a joint articulation of what can be seen and heard. They are organic mixtures of movement and sound produced in the instant of a gesture. Acoustic drawings conform to a musical notion of time. The latter defines the limits of the action, whose specific characteristic is continuity. However, musical time was eliminated once I entered a soundproof chamber... There was no echo whatsoever there, the tiniest movement could be heard, our breath, this and nothing besides. It was suddenly no longer necessary to create musical time, because it already existed. I know that John Cage had a similar experience, which he describes in his book *Pour les oiseaux...*[4] As far as my acoustic drawings are concerned, I wouldn't like them to be considered as either music or concrete music. The most exact way of describing them would be as "acoustic art."

It appears that you are an outsider in the Czech scene...

Yes, that's right. I am an atypical, and very isolated Czech artist, on the fringe of the Prague scene, in particular. Art has almost always been dominated by outside influence here. The epigones of surrealism, among others, have served to lend the Prague scene its present character, this excessive turmoil, this surplus of soul. I remain a Czech artist, however, and I identify myself as such, along with certain traditions of this country where I have my roots. During the Second World War, in 1942, I began my studies at the School of Applied Arts in Brno. A unique place! This institution operated along the lines of the Bauhaus. The teachers there were all key figures in the Devetsil movement. Our teacher, the architect Frantisek Kalivoda, had selected one of the first monographs on Moholy-Nagy as a study manual, a work which had been published under his name in the review "Téléhor" in 1936. Where else in Europe did they offer a teaching program like that? It wasn't to be found in Prague, or Paris for that matter!

What were the repercussions of this shock wave?

There was no shock wave. On the contrary, all this seemed natural and familiar to me. During the thirties, we had been receiving

(4)—*Pour les oiseaux,* Interviews with Daniel Charles at the Musée d'Art Moderne in Paris, 1970, Editions Belfond, Paris, 1976.

reviews at home, like "Panorama," "Zijeme," and "Druzstevni Praze," founded and put together by the famous designer Ladislav Sutnar, who emigrated to the United States. These were the most avant-garde reviews available at that time. Thanks to one of his publications, my father had acquired a very modern carpet, featuring a line drawing made up of geometric motifs. I still can picture it in my memory right before me now. It was very beautiful, and I realize today that this carpet forms the framework, the thread of my whole oeuvre. Luckily, I have kept a drawing of it which I did when I was fifteen, and it is as if I drew it only yesterday.

Sometimes, you are considered alongside the Fluxus artists by mistake. However, aren't you similar to some of them, a "performer"?

The mechanical birds and the musical spinning top gave a new dimension to my acoustic drawings. They extended the aleatory data of the process. It was impossible to determine their exact trajectory or predict the duration of their movement. During the course of a performance, my role is that of an actor, almost a spectator. There is an element of magic, a chance score, an order hidden within the chaos. Every one of these acoustic and mechanical drawings is a kind of miniature happening, a living spectacle full of surprise and poetry, rich in sound effects. The mere fact of having staged some of them in public has itself provided great stimulus for me. I was everything all at once, an illusionist, a musician and choreographer. I would stand in the dark in front of a table where I was about to draw, holding a black hat in my hand, then strike a match and light a candle (which was sometimes hidden in the oval box for my top hat, out of which the glow of candlelight could be seen). I did this for the first time in Prague and in Poland during the seventies. The audience burst out with laughter, and it was very pleasing to see people enjoying themselves. Once the mirth had died down a little, I caught their attention again by ringing a bell, or by setting a clockwork frog in motion—my best percussionist. When this had finished, I showed the drawing to the audience. All of a sudden, the laughter stopped

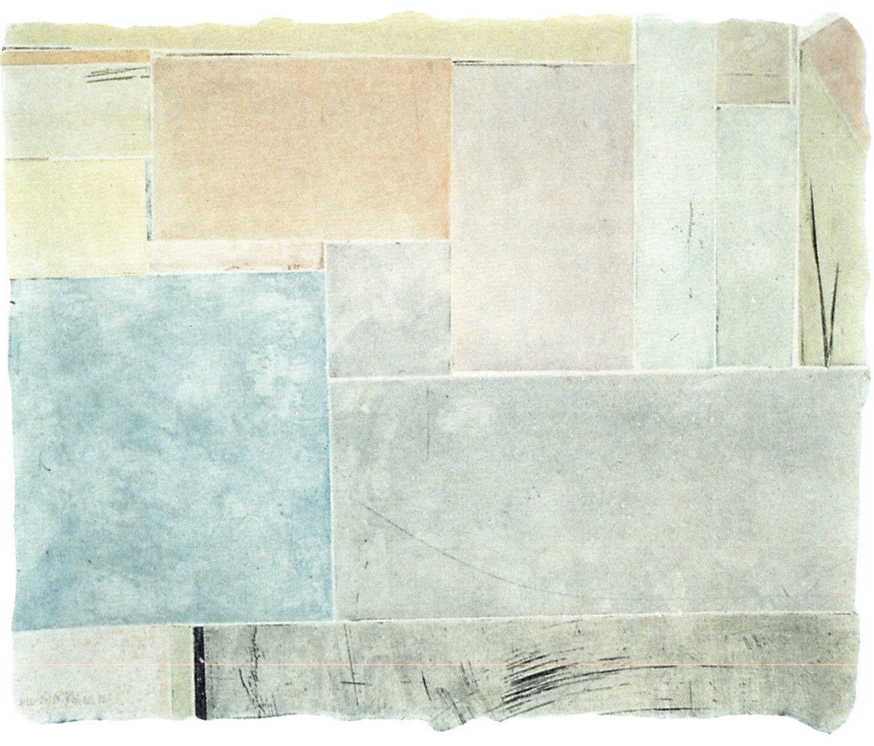

21 - John Cage, *HV2*, 1992
(n°24 of a series of 15 related color etchings in 3 impressions each—Handmade Abaca—
11-1/2 x 14-1/2")

The title of John Cage's new series, *HV2*, refers to horizontal/vertical and *HV*, an earlier series of monotypes also based on the right angle. For the fifteen images that comprise *HV2*, Cage arranged small copper plates "improvisationally," either in a horizontal or vertical direction, so that they fit tightly within the dimensions of the deckle-edged, handmade paper. All of the copper plates were fragments Cage found around the studio and the number of plates that comprise each print is indicated in the title. The plates bore marks of wear, an occasional "x" (a registration mark from a previous project), and, perhaps, grease or tarnish, all of which were retained and valued by Cage. Each plate was covered with a lightly etched aquatint to hold the tone and protect what was already on the plate. The color of each geometric area is a mixture of between one and six of the 64 pigments and/or inks on hand. The choice of color in all cases was determined by chance operations based on the I Ching charts Cage uses for all his decision-making. Because of the light etch, the overall color palette tends toward pastel. (From the *Crown Point Press Release*)

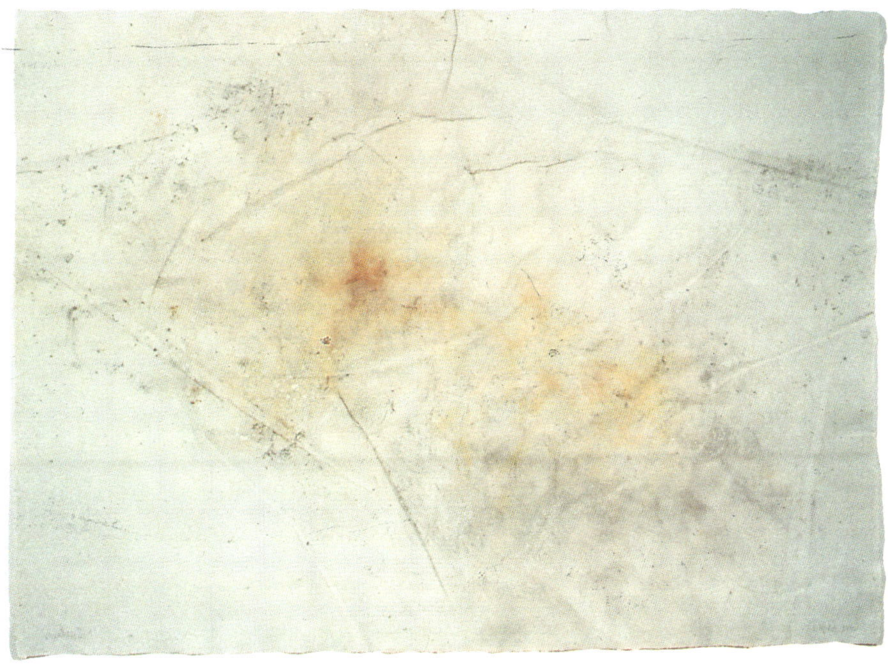

22 - John Cage, *Variations III*, 1992

(n°8 of a series of 57 monotypes, branding on smoked paper—Roma Tiziano (light grey) and Roma del Sarto (dark grey)—17 1/2 x 25 3/4")

Variations III, so named because it relates to two earlier *Variation* series Cage has made at the Crown Point Press, is printed on two shades of warm grey Roma paper (originally used for Cage's *Global Village* etchings of 1989). As in the earlier *Variation* prints, Cage asked the printers to "smoke' the paper using the method Cage devised in 1985 at the press. The printers set aflame a wad of newspapers and then placed dampened paper on the fire to extinguish it. The smoke and occasional burn marks is recorded differently on each sheet. Next, Cage branded the sheets with a heated circular iron ring and/or iron bar, again using the I Ching charts to determine the number of brands and their placement. He predetermined that the bar could be used a maximum of three times, and the ring placed on the paper flatly or on its side once each, so that at most a sheet might contain five brand marks. He also allowed for the possibility of no marks. The paper was not flattened at Cage's request. Cage thinks of the creases as an intriguing three-dimensional element. There are 57 images in the series; the number was determined by the amount of paper available. (From the *Crown Point Press Release*) **(© D.R.)**

and the audience fell deadly serious. Some musicians then climbed on to the stage and "played" the drawing as if they were interpreting a score. To begin with, I had no idea my acoustic drawings could form a basis for an instrumental performance. I had never thought of them as scores. This instrumental aspect became apparent to me when Anestis Logothetis payed me a visit.

Recordings of your acoustic drawings are frequently compared to concrete music. Wouldn't you say that this resemblance is only superficial?

According to Pierre Schaeffer, every single sound is the reflection of an event. In this case, the acoustic drawing and the recording thereof conform to a given program, which is chosen in advance. Some recordings are destined to be rearranged in the laboratory, without receiving further interference from outside, according to precise indications given on the drawing itself. Others function simply by means of strict superimposition of sounds onto a single magnetic tape. The form contained in the recording does not correspond to what can be heard live, for it tends to integrate the objective, and generally accepted conditions prevailing at the time of the sound recording: the acoustic qualities of the recording space, the position and relative distances between the microphones situated around the sound sources, or even outside the studio altogether. What can be heard, therefore, is the humming of the spinning top and the spasms of its disequilibrium, whereas outside, you might hear the unexpected wailing of a siren, serving as an echo to the humming...

On seeing you working, I had the impression that your plastic and sonorous works bordered on something which is not all that removed from architecture.

Painting raises essential questions. The most fundamental of these, in my opinion, concerns the third dimension, the problem of depth. According to Gilles Deleuze, the third dimension is not added from outside to the length and to the breadth, but remains a hidden creative principle operating behind these two dimensions. I proposed my own solution to this problem with tactile drawings. This involved a slow process of maturing, which began in 1966 and ended three years later. Ink drawings were followed by graphic scores, upon which I began to make acoustic drawings blindly, without seeing anything, just by touch. I would clear away everything from around me, keeping nothing but a screen of white paper, through which I passed my arms and legs. I drew with my bare hands on this sort of drum skin stretched in space, so that there was nothing but the body and the echo of the body, sound. At the same time, this was also an open, and endlessly reopened drawing. When finished, I would tear it up and take the work with me. The surface of the paper would bear nothing but an empty circle, the size of a man, in which one's gaze is drawn, towards infinity. Another piece, *Kroky,* anticipated the space-sound. Ideally closed up in a sleeve of canvas, the spectator listens to my footsteps passing across the monumental drawings.

What were your relations, your contacts with Western artistic circles?

Although my work is isolated from the mainstream of Czechoslovakian art, it has nevertheless always been constantly confronted with the latest developments there, and fuelled by fortunate sources of dialogue. Joseph Beuys and I were in very close contact. There was a kinship of spirit between us, as if we had been fellow students at the Academy. Our contact broke off when he asked me to join the DSP, the political party he had helped to found.

In Gand I met Mario Merz... Composers and musicians also visited me in my studio in Prague, including Erhard Karkoschka, Anestis Logothetis, Jean-Yves Bosseur and also Tom Marioni from Los Angeles, whose work is very similar in nature to the principles of acoustic drawing. I find these same principles in the last watercolors painted by John Cage at the Mountain Lake Workshop. Despite the span of thirty years separating us, we had parallel intuitions...

(Prague/Paris, 1992)*

* Fragments of an interview with Milan Grygar on the subject of his acoustic drawings, which represent only one part of his artistic activity.

23 - John Cage, *Without Horizon*,1992
(n°12 of a series of 57 related, unique prints, drypoint and etching on smoked paper—Handmade Abaca—7-1/2 x 8-1/2")

Without Horizon, the third series of etchings completed in 1992, reminded Cage of landscape, and the title refers to a mesostic written earlier. Deciding to stay with the number 57, the number of images in *Variations III*, Cage chose 57 edges of 13 stones, stones he has used as templates in former etchings. Using spitbite, sugarlift, softground, hardground, drypoint and one of 36 brushes or several improvised or traditional drawing tools, Cage drew along the edge of a stone rather than around the contour as he has done previously. The technique, brush, and particular stone edge were all chosen through chance operations. Cage concentrated his marks on the lower third of each small piece of handmade, smoked paper (coincidentally 57 pieces) and limited the number of lines on each print to three, four or five.
(From the *Crown Point Press Release*) **(© D.R.)**

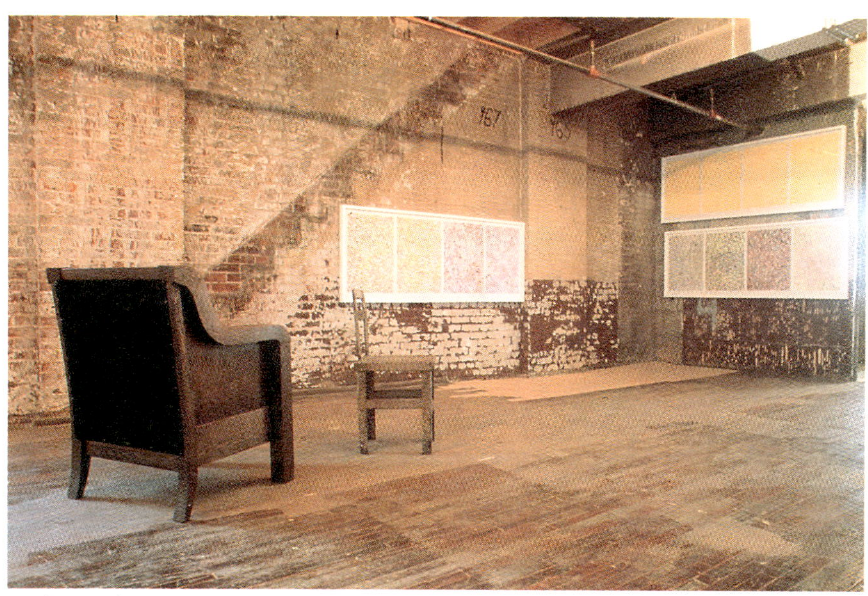

24 - Changing Installation at the Mattress Factory, John Cage, 1991

"in an empty room the chair(s), the walls neither painted nor the paint removed (the walls as they are), the use of chance operations to determine the placement and orientation of the chair(s) and which fifteen of a source of forty-eight works, twelve each by Dove Bradshaw, John Cage, Mary Jean Kenton, Marsha Skinner, are presented each day in which positions "
Above, three paintings by Mary Jean Kenton: *Poetry Which Obviously Makes No Sound* (left), *Resistance Drawn Up Where The Flowers Inform* (upper right), *Nomadic Of Direct Involvement* (lower right). **(© D.R.)**

CHAPTER VI

John Cage and the Visual

John Cage's *Theater Piece* (1960) is particularly representative of an artistic movement which aims to consider visual and auditive experiences as always more necessarily imbricated, in a logic of intensifying relations which seems somehow to emerge of itself.

In *Theater Piece*, each performer (one to eight can execute the score) composes his or her own repertoire of visual and acoustic actions by writing twenty freely chosen nouns and/or verbs on twenty numbered slips of paper. These are the elements which will subsequently be brought into play. Thus the numbers written on the score correspond to a program of actions whose duration will be defined according to their inscription in the space of the page. Several numbers being combined for each action, the actor/musicians find themselves confronted by what are sometimes very complex situations, which can lead them to simultaneously intermingle up to a hundred types of different actions. Obviously, each version of *Theater Piece* varies greatly from all the others.

Highly dynamic in the United States, this tendency to regard the world as a theater, to defy the scissions between artistic disciplines and specializations, is certainly not foreign to the experiments of Marcel Duchamp, Laszlo Moholy-Nagy, and Kurt Schwitters, during the first half of this century.

Through the processes he develops, John Cage works in such a way that each mode of activity gains in specificity, yet without being forced to submit to any preestablished definition. His musical, graphic, or poetic "actions" are certainly not to be evaluated by reciprocal comparison. Although both his *Plexigrams* and his *Variations*, for example, were realized using transparent materials— which could liken them to works by Robert Rauschenberg based precisely on the use of impressions atop transparent panels between which the visitor can wander—still these works present marked divergences in nature: unaccompanied by indications for possible acoustic manifestations, would they be plastic objects? Has Cage not introduced into his books, for example into the volume *M*, certain pages which are related to visual poetry? If doubt reigns permanently over the definition of Cage's activities—and the possibility of any definition —it nonetheless remains clearly affirmed that each experience is to be assumed in its autonomy, in full knowledge of its specific functional rules, whether those of writing, listening, playing, looking, or reading. No experience can take precedence over another: they are all in a certain way irreducible. In Cage's practice, one phenomenon never definitively disappears to let another take its place, no more than an individual must necessarily renounce his identity to let another personality predominate. Beyond all hierarchies, the putting into practice of anarchy on a ludic scale is one of the fundamental teachings conveyed by the *modus operandi* of John Cage.

Indeed, Cage's music and thought have been and remain central for several generations of European and American artists. As so clearly shown by the numerous references to his creative personality across texts and interviews, his work marks a turning point in music and more generally in contemporary art, due to the innovative methods of writing which he has elaborated and which continue to demystify the image of the composer. Cage is an inventor. He experiments with existing instruments—as in the case of the prepared piano—or he explores new modes of notation and communication with the potential to explode the rigid character of the artwork, whether it be musical, plastic, or poetic in nature. Extending beyond the auditively privileged zone of the concert, his attitude aims to render us more receptive and reactive toward our environment. He

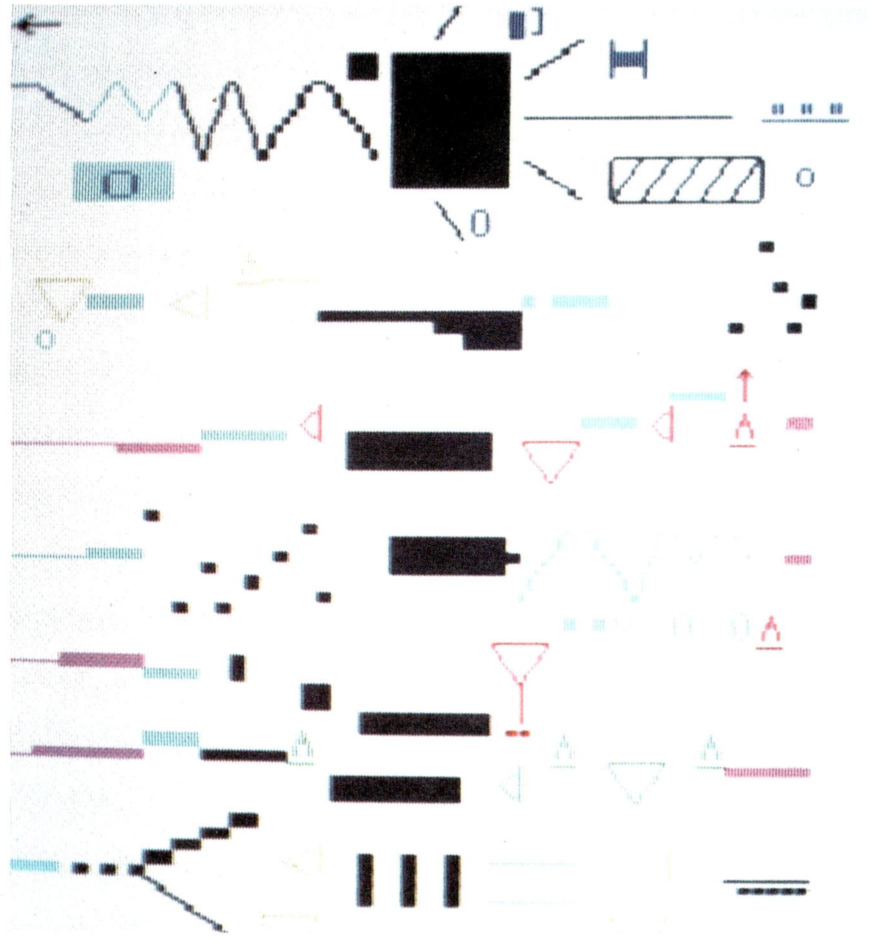

25 - Francis Miroglio, *Mosaïques 7*, 1985

"Graphic music conceived in 1985 for violin, clarinet, trumpet, saxophone, trombone, bass, percussion. This score is meant to be viewed, but could also be interpreted by instrumentalists.
It endeavours to stir the reader's imagination while urging him to focus it on structured zones.
By including every single graphic symbol on a chart of squares previously designed on the screen, the telematic ("Minitel") technique returns across the centuries to the art of mosaics, but adds a kinetic element; by spacing out of the signs, it includes the notion of time.
Some of the features of music may be rediscovered in the reading: its dynamic, the poetical impact of a trajectory ". F. M.
(First presented at the exhibition 'Les Immatériaux' organized by Jean-François Lyotard at the Centre Georges Pompidou on 29 March 1985).(© D.R.)

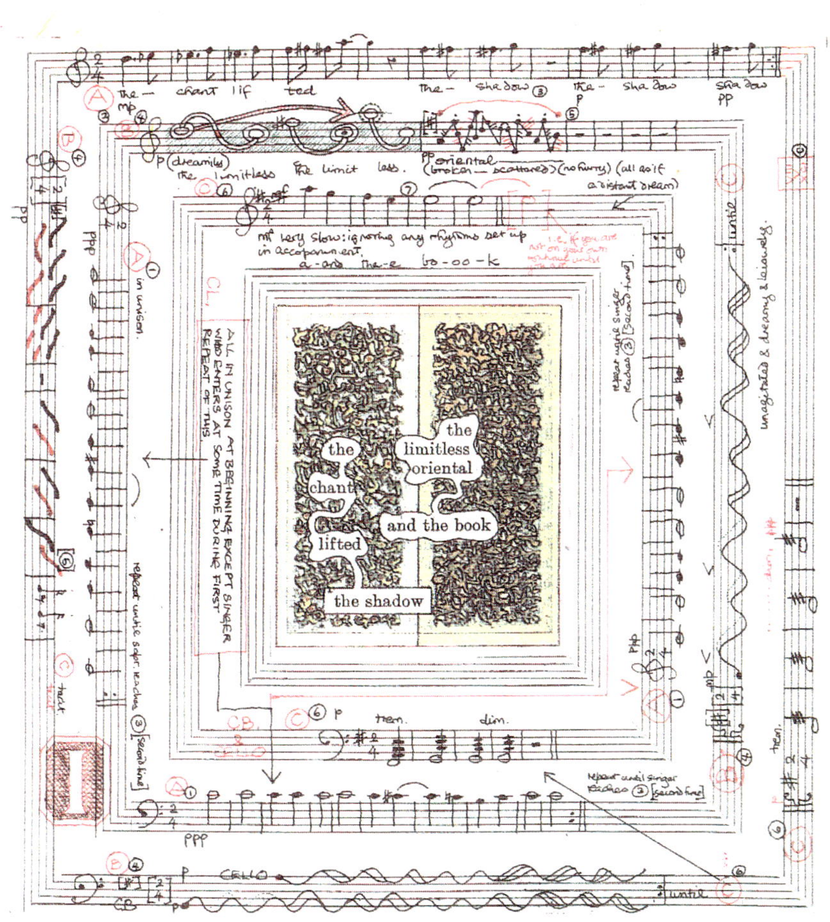

26 - Tom Phillips, *Six of Hearts*, 1991
(One of the six scores realized for Mary Wiegold)
(© D.R.)

has often been judged, in a simplistic way, as a provoker of scandals (the *4'33"* of silence, to cite one of his most famous compositions). Yet in his approach, art and philosophy (above all Zen Buddhism, an important element in his reflection) are inseparable, just as in his activity, life and art tend to become one.

John Cage

Do you consider your activities as a composer and a visual artist as independent, or do they act upon each other?

I expected that something done in graphic art could be done in musical composition, but I discovered, somewhat to my surprise, that what is horizontal in graphic art needs to be vertical in musical work. That is: the horizon is important to the eye, but time is important to the ear.

Have you tried this sort of relationship in your etchings?

Yes. And there I used the horizontal, but when I worked with the music, I had to use the vertical.

Which works are you referring to?

The graphic works were the series of etchings called *Undersurface* and the musical work was *Thirty Pieces for Five Orchestras.*

Your visual work seems to be rather recent; for instance, Not Wanting to Say Anything About Marcel *is from '69, you began printmaking in '78, and water colours in '88.*

Before I studied with Schoenberg I also did some painting, but I painted more or less in an early stage, simply squinting and deciding what color something was; I was just looking at nature and trying to paint what I saw. But when I met Schoenberg, and asked him to be my teacher, he said: "Will you devote your life to music?" I said "Yes," and then he agreed. So I abandoned graphic work until much later. Actually, until just after the death of Marcel Duchamp. I happened to be with Jasper Johns when we were both asked to make some work about Duchamp, and Jasper said: "I don't want to say anything about Marcel." So I called my work: *Not Wanting to Say Anything About Marcel.*

So it was the death of Marcel Duchamp which provoked you to do more visual works?

Yes.

You have invented many "graphic stimulations" in your notation, for pieces like Cartridge Music, *the* Piano Concerto, *and the* Variations. *Were your preocupations exclusively musical, or also visual and spatial?*

They were musical. But since I made those notations, it brought about people to ask me to do graphic work.

So it encouraged you?

No, it encouraged other people to ask me to do something. It was actually Alice Weston in Cincinnati who asked me to do a series of works which became *Not Wanting to Say...*

But before, you didn't think about it?

I did actually have an exhibition of my manuscripts in the Stable Gallery, at a time when Bob Rauschenberg had an exhibit in the same gallery. But I thought of it as music notation, and it was used as music notation; I didn't think of it as painting. However, since it was shown in the galleries, some of the pages of the manuscripts sold, and I was obliged to copy them very carefully in order to keep them as music!

Are there any links which might connect your activities as a visual artist and a sound artist? I am thinking for instance of the method of the I Ching... What kinds of methods make these passages from one activity to another possible for you?

The asking of questions, and the receiving of answers from the I Ching. The questions have to do with space in the case of graphic work, and with time in the case of music, as I said before. However, I was able to take the page of the music notation as though it were blank, but potentially music, and treat it graphically, but with the idea of the vertical taking the place of the horizontal. In the case of the etchings, I discovered the relation between numbers and the page that I am working on. If I work in a grid of 64 x 64, the amount of space given to a horizontal unit can be different from the amount of space given to a vertical unit, and so I can locate a point in a rectangle, or several points; then I can have an intersection of the horizontal and the vertical, and at that point, if I am making a drawing, I can place a stone. If I am making a piece of music, as I did for Joëlle Leandre, I can make a musical notation of it; but if what I write goes from left to right, it can't go from right back to left, because of the nature of music, which is to proceed in time.

Did you use, for instance, the magic square? I believe you did in the past, for some of your scores.

That was a long time ago.

But you didn't use it for your visual works?

No.

Do you integrate sounds into your visual works?

No, I used stones, for instance, to draw circular forms, but I didn't make sounds with the stones.

You never integrated the two?

Only in the process of working: that is to say I've made etchings with stones, and I've made music with stones, but they're two different pieces.

What are your favorite techniques: drawing, etching, dry-point? Or does it depend on the moment?

I like the one I am doing, whatever it may be.

Could it be oil, for instance?

I haven't tried that, except when I was much younger; I remember that one had the problem of drying time. I like drawing very much, and particularly the fact that the work is finished, once it is drawn. In some of the processes of etching there is a period of waiting, but watercolor is also done quite quickly.

You like this sort of immediacy, this instantaneousness?

It's extremely convenient. And the other thing that is difficult about graphic work in general is that it needs a studio, whereas music I can write at a table. In New York it would be awkward for me to have a studio as an artist and to write at home as a composer, so I go once a year to Crown Point Press in California, and I go less often and less regularly to make watercolors in Virginia.

Do you prepare yourself for the things you'll be working on? I mean, when you know that you will be in San Francisco in February, do you prepare ideas, or do you just let things happen when you are in the studio?

I do both. I dream about ideas, and then when I'm in the studio, they often change in relation to what is practical.

But these dreams...

Provoke action.

What kinds of dreams are they? Are they meditations on natural elements or processes?

More like processes.

Indeed, you have written that you are more interested in processes than in objects, but when you carry out a drawing, don't you produce a fixed object? When you do music it can change anytime, but the etching will always be there.

I think that sets me making the next one, because then it's different from the first one!

So you immediately project another one...

Yes. Then you could have two and look only at one at a time.

The letter seems to be important in your work. Is it because it's common to various forms of expression: poetry, music, graphic art? It can be read, heard, or seen. You mentioned Not Wanting to Say Anything About Marcel; *was this work made with letters?*

Yes, and since Marcel had died, I thought of letting the letters graphically lose some of their parts, and later I was very happy to read a remark of Marcel Duchamp, to the effect that he enjoyed looking at signs that were outdoors and that had suffered rain and so forth, so that when the letters were changed, he could imagine what they had been. He enjoyed that.

But for yourself, the letter is a kind of bridge between activities, because it can be sung, or it can be shown visually...

That's true.

When you begin a project like your "mesostics," do you know right from the start whether it will be sung, inscribed in a score, inscribed in a book, or shown at an exhibition? Do you know the nature of the project?

I don't think so. That comes later. In the case of the mesostics, I have the letter of the name or of the subject. I must say that I don't think about publication when I'm writing; it comes later, after the writing is finished.

Certain pages of your book M *can't be pronounced before an audience; it's a kind of visual poetry. So when you do it, you know that it won't be a score.*

I'm thinking of it as poetry, yes. And I like the look of the mesostics on the page. On some occasions, I decide to make a song of certain mesostics, but I haven't done that with all of them. *Roaratorio* was created from *Writing through Finnegan's Wake.*

But you don't have any precise reason to decide that a given mesostic will be integrated to...

No, I think that those concerns and goals appear later, after the writing is finished.

Morton Feldman used the expression "between categories" for some cases of ambiguous artistic activities. Do you consider your work as between categories? Do you like the expression?

I could accept it; I don't think I would have said it. I wouldn't think in terms of categories. I'm thinking of another person, Dick Higgins, who would think of media.

Yes, he used the word "intermedia." But you wouldn't use it either...

I don't think so. I would say writing for writing and music for music, and then I would distinguish between etchings, drawings, and watercolors.

Does time play as important a role in the realization of a graphic work as it does in the definition of a musical process?

No, it doesn't in the case of drawing. My inclination with my graphic work is to do the work, and not to look at the clock.

Ah! I wasn't thinking about the clock, but about a kind of subjective time.

But I think that time is clock time. When I was in Russia, I met the composer Sofia Goubaïdulina, and when she saw that I was using watches and clocks for the performance of music, she said: "You must remember that there is an inner clock." So I made a piece thinking of her, a variation of my piece *4'33"* according to my inner clock. Along with other variations, it turned out to be something between 12' and 13' of silence.

That's your inner time?

That was what I used in that case; it would be another time if the performance were another day. But my inner clock seems to go slower than clock time.

Natural elements—the four elements, and stone as well—seem important in your graphic productions. Does this type of work bring you to feel a special relationship with nature? It's true that in your music, there is perhaps also a relationship to nature, but it seems more pronounced in your graphic work.

Yes, a bit more. In the 30s, when I was much younger, I met two artists: Maurice Graves and Marc Tobey. Marc Tobey changed my way of seeing during a walk in Seattle. We walked very slowly, and he pointed out all the various things that he was noticing, that he could see. After that walk my way of looking changed, so that later I was able to look at the white paintings of Robert Rauschenberg and see that they were not entirely white, but that the dust and so forth was falling on them. Tobey was able to see everything, he noticed everything.

What about Maurice Graves?

Maurice Graves comes close to nature in another way. But in a way that resembles poetry rather than visuality. I like both.

Some of your titles sound Japanese: Haiku, Ryoanji, Ryoku. *Is there any reason, any precise intention behind this?*

Yes, it's consciously involved with Japanese culture. Both with the poetry, and with the gardens. In Japanese gardens there are fifteen stones, so that when I made an etching called *The Missing Stone*, it was an etching with fourteen stones rather than fifteen: one was missing. In the case of *haiku* and *renga* poetry, the number seventeen is of great importance.

Is calligraphy important for you?

No, I don't think of my graphic work as involving gesture. I'm beginning to sense the possibility of gesture through the use of a brush in watercolors, but I don't feel gifted in terms of gesture.

You don't feel like an instrumentalist.

Right. So I use rocks to make curves, I use rulers to make straight lines, and I use compasses to make circles.

Perhaps because these objects are a bit neutral, I mean, it's not your ability that counts...

It's not my gesture. It's not my signature.

That aspect is also present in your musical processes, where you go beyond your subjective choices. Ryoanji *is the title of a piece of music, as well as the title of four dry-points. What are the relationships between the two projects?*

The *Ryoanji* drawings and the score both use the same rocks; I made circles around them in the case of the drawings, as I said earlier, and I did not draw all the way around them in the case of the music, but only from left to right. However, the stones have been placed in the notation areas for the music, they've been placed as though in a space.

And you used this approach in your score for double bass as well... So you use it to obtain curves of some kind?

Yes. It's a music of *glissandi.*

That's why it can be played by different instrumental ensembles, because I believe there are a few versions of Ryoanji*?*

There are about eight, I think.

Transparency also seems to play an active part both in some of your scores (again, Cartridge Music, Variations...*) and also in your visual works, for instance* Plexigrams. *You did some of the work more or less at the same time as Rauschenberg, I think. Did you discuss this use of transparent material with him?*

No, I think that he did it first, but I don't think that I was aware of his work when I did it myself.

Did you discuss with him?

No.

Do you think you had the same reasons to do it?

I imagine so. When I first met Bob Rauschenberg, we both had a sense of not needing to talk, because we understood one another, so there was no inclination to talk. I think he would have said what I was saying to myself, so to speak!

Do you find it interesting to use transparency in order to see something which is not in the work, but which is behind it?

Yes, it's very interesting. I think our experience now is one of reflections and transparencies and collage: that is, of seeing several things at once. When we look at one thing, if we look at this drawing on the wall, for example, we also see the curtains, we see other things than what we think we are looking at, so that our experience is to see many things at once.

It's a new sense of polyphony...

I think so.

You have done collages both in your visual monotypes and in your music, for example, in Fontana Mix. *Is your approach very different when you do collage with sounds or with visual elements?*

No, I don't think so. The only difference I have perceived is the one I already mentioned, which is the importance of the vertical in music, and the importance of the horizontal in the visual arts. Both are extremely important to Robert Rauschenberg in his painting: the vertical *and* the horizontal. His paintings are almost intersections. Very curiously, like Mondrian, but from a representational point of experience.

Not the diagonals?

No. Not so strongly, either with Rauschenberg or with Mondrian.

And what is the diagonal for you?

When you mention it, it makes me think of dancing. The diagonal is important in theatrical dancing because it's a longer line than either the vertical or the horizontal.

Some of your recent works have been done in collaboration with other artists, for instance Calvin Sumpsian. Do you consider these artists as performers?

In the case of Calvin Sumpsian I was able to give him directions, since as a composer, I am familiar with giving directions to a musician.

I gave him similar directions, and I accepted his performance.

But have you done visual work with other people? The etchings, for instance—do you do them alone?

I do them with the help of people at the press. They know how to do things I don't know how to do.

But as you are a musician, how do you see them?

In the case of the etchings, I see them as performers. I don't say "put this at this point," but "put this in this general direction," so that there will be several right placements.

You look for a multiplicity of responses...

Of possibilities.

So it resembles your scores, in a way.

Well, I have directions and I actually transmit them to the printer verbally. So I don't make a score, except for myself.

It's a fugitive score.

Yes.

Do you enjoy the act of drawing the musical signs?

I no longer do my own copy. I have a copyist. That happened quite some time ago. But until the sixties, my music wasn't published and I did all my own copy.

But for anyone who looks at the scores, very great care seems to have been given to the letters and the signs.

Yes. But the nature of the musical manuscript is such that if your eyes are not as good as they were, it's more difficult. I began by having glasses, and I've ended by having a copyist!

But what you do visually is very precise.

Well, I like that. I enjoyed it.

The way you did your scores recalls the care that Satie lavished on his notation.

Right. He did it so very beautifully.

It's not very far from yourself in a way.

Thank you very much.

But you didn't do it consciously?

I suppose the real answer is yes and no. I enjoyed the look of the notation on the page, but as a result, I made manuscripts which sometimes approached the condition of lace because I took a razor blade and cut out all the part of the paper that I didn't want. And unlike Stravinsky, I used prepared paper with staves, and then I had to cut out the stuff that I didn't use. He only drew the stuff that he was going to use, and I did that in the *Piano Solo* too, I simply drew what I wanted. But many of my manuscripts are written on printed staves.

At this time, did you use specific pens, papers, or inks?

Yes.

The papers were very important, for instance, because of the imperfections.

Yes. But as I pointed out in a talk at the Darmstadt Festival, the principle of the imperfections does not make one sheet of paper more important than another, because each sheet has its own imperfections. And there I use the principle of time, to give me a certain amount of time in which to look for imperfections: I would say, "I can look for imperfections for one minute," or "I can look for five minutes..."

Could it be more?

No, mostly it was done in order to get through it quickly.

Because the I Ching was very slow, the I Ching decisions are very difficult to do and very slow.

Well, no longer for me, because I have it in the computer. They were slow until around 1960, and now they're quite fast!

Does it change your approach to the I Ching?

No.

In 1964, you wrote : "It's predictable that the new music will be answered by a new painting, one which we have not yet seen." Do you still have this feeling today?

Well, I'm interested in music as you know, and I'm interested in art, and I'm for instance very interested in the painting of Mary Jean Kenton. She lives near Pittsburgh. She makes rectangles with water colors or with other techniques, they can be oil or acrylic, or one thing or another; she makes them of different sizes and different colors, and then packages them in envelopes. It may be a painting having fifty or a hundred pieces, and those pieces can go together in any relationship, and can change from day to day. I enjoy the experience of her work very much. An art critic whose name is not clear in my mind uses the term "visuality" with regard to her work, and this has made me search without success for a similar term that would apply to sound. But I haven't found a really satisfactory one: "audiality," for instance, isn't interesting as a word. What Mary Jane Kenton's painting exercises is the ability to see: that is what I want in a painting and that is perhaps what I meant in the remark that you quoted. We always want the experiences we live to be the experience of seeing immediately, as though we hadn't seen before. Or as I put it in other cases: to live as a tourist.

For you, to be a tourist is to be aware of everything that is happening, to be able to catch things?

Yes. To see and to hear as though you were seeing or hearing for the first time.

Do you have other visual projects?

I'm here in Munich to make a film, and the film makes use of a live program which has been designed by Andrew Calver. He worked with me on *Europeras 1, 2, 3, 4,* and *5.* He does all of my programming.

What is the process for this film?

It's light. I don't know exactly how many lights there are, but it's nearly a hundred. They're not used at once, but it makes a light situation which changes, and the cameraman has his changes of lenses, and so forth.

So you have done a score of the lights.

Yes. Well, we have done a process which leads to it.

Is it an abstract film?

Very realistic. But there is no plot. There are variations of white, black, and gray.

So that's a sort of extension of what you do with etchings or other media.

Yes.

Did you do something like this before?

We've had installations of light in the case of a poem which is called *Mesostics and Writings Through the Essay on the Duty of Disobedience of Henry David Thoreau.* When the music is played—which involves 36 loudspeakers—then the lights in a darkened room are slowly changing, so that as you listen to the sounds, you can see the changes of lights.

In this case, one could say there is a fusion of poetry, music, and visuality. And how would you call it?

Visuality.

So that's visuality for you!

Yes, that word works. I haven't found a word for music. As I said, the work of Mary Jean Kenton impressed me very much, because it omits the idea of composition and insists upon freshness (or uniqueness); you could even say, on the physicality of looking. And now in my music I am looking for a similar experience in sound, and that's why I am so anxious to find a word which works as well as visuality does for graphic art.

You mean a sort of physicality?

A physical experience, in fact: the enjoyment of listening.

Which is not a sort of narcissism...

No, it's entirely realistic, and that's what I do: wherever I am, I listen to the sounds of the environment without any idea of composition, but with the enjoyment of the experience of listening.

A sort of penetration of the sounds?

Yes. I wish I could remember phrases in the third chapter of *Ulysses* of Joyce, in the very first sentence of the third chapter, where he speaks of the experience of looking, and in the second paragraph, of the experience of hearing. This is so important to life: the eyes and the ears.

Together?

Or separately.

You don't necessarily try for a fusion of the two?

No. I do as I have done with the dance of Merce Cunningham: I try to keep a separation between the two. Just as we do when we see reflections and transparencies. We have the pleasure of seeing, of a multiple experience, a rich experience.

(Munich, April 26, 1992)

CHAPTER VII

Intermedia

In place of the word "mixed media"—designating manifestations such as light shows where the visual and acoustic domains are most often simply stuck one atop the other—Dick Higgins advances the notion of "intermedia" to evoke practices where a veritable fusion is effected between several fields of activity.

In the article "De Joan Miró à Francis Miroglio—Graphique de la projection," Daniel Charles writes: "After the first 'happening' organized by J. Cage at Black Mountain College in 1952, multimedia works proliferated; their taxonomy soon began to pose problems. Which categories should be used to identify them? This question was not only of academic interest; according to the degree of integration or homogenization of the different components in play, the content of the event to be appreciated varied. Finally, the classification suggested in 1973 by Stanley Gibb gained widespread acceptance: he contrasted multimedia, which respects the autonomy of essentially distinct elements in confrontation—sound, decor, stage movement, image, gesture, smell—to 'mixed-media' pieces, tending toward an 'equalization of ingredients' (without however undertaking their hierarchization), and also to 'intermedia' works, which pursue the ideal of a rigorous interdependence of the diverse components.[1]"

If the activities of the Fluxus group presented numerous cases of interferences between artistic practices, the intermedia experiments of the late 1960s were more deliberately anchored in reality, linked to specific contents, and more individualized as well. So it is with George

(1) — Daniel Charles, in "Cahiers du C.R.E.M", n°6/7, 1987-88, p. 99.

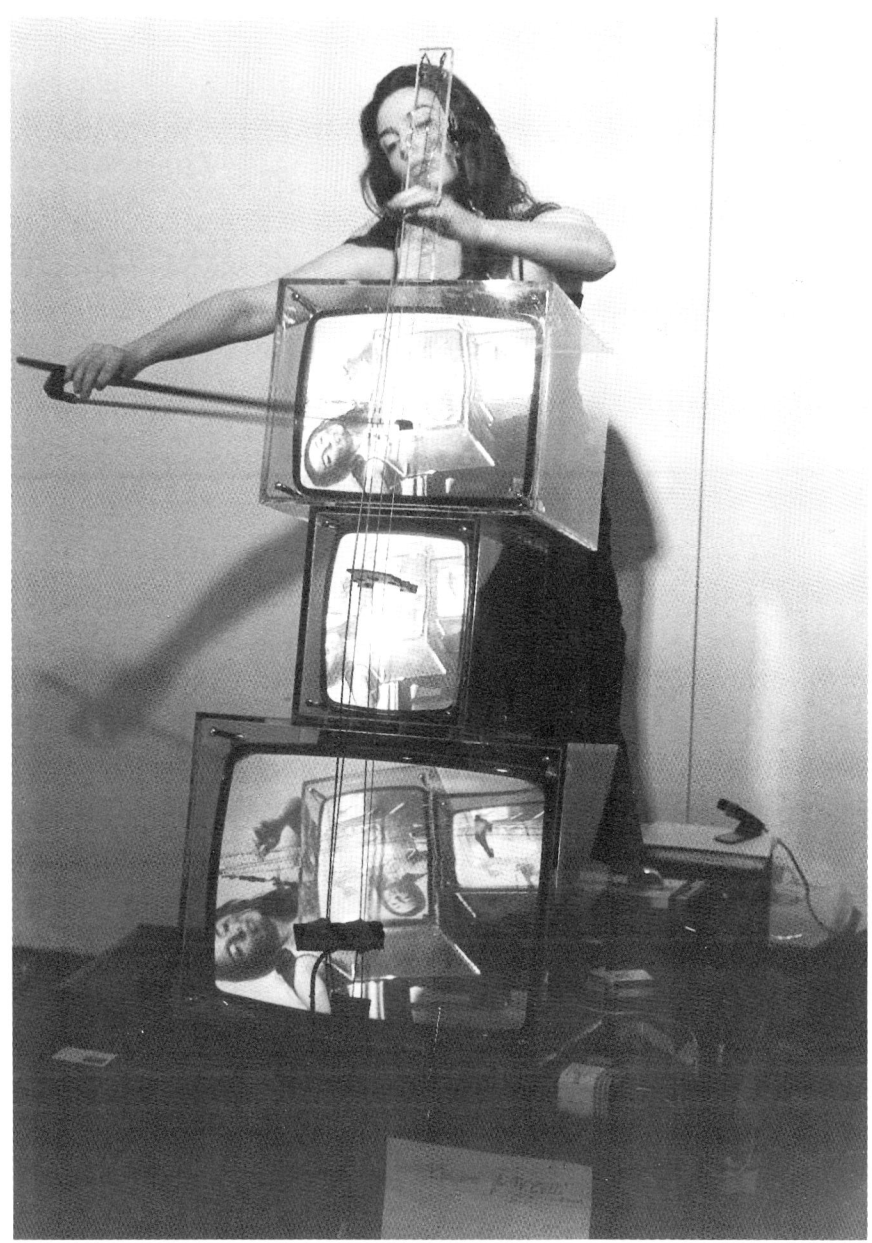

27 - Nam June Paik, *TV-Cello*
(with Charlotte Moorman)
photo by Hanns Sohm Markgröningen (© D.R.)

Brecht's "events"—kinds of "overall poly-sensorial experiences"—or Wolf Vostell's "*dé-coll/ages*," where the public "learns to live and to undergo the psychological test of the environment," life and the human body being considered here as full-fledged art forms. This is also the case in the "actions" and "environments" of Joseph Beuys.

A feeling of ephemerality and impermanence reigned—in a resolutely conceptual sense—over the proposals of La Monte Young and Kosugi in the early sixties, whereas the "video-laser" interventions of David Tudor and Lowell Cross, the installations of Nam June Paik, and the environment-oriented creations of Alvin Lucier sprang from a manipulation of the most sophisticated technological resources.

Thus Alvin Lucier created "multimedia" pieces, including "video environments" with recorded and live images, voices, composed and improvised music, and so forth. Often requiring the participation of several interpreters—a fact which led him to call *Perfect Lives* an opera—these pieces have an incontestable dimension of "performance," both by the artist and his partners.

In most of the multimedia projects the establishment of an audio-visual circuit becomes an integral part of the composition, contributing to the identity of each project in the same way as the definition of plastic materials or musical instrumentations.

The central figure of this form of artistic activity is assuredly Nam June Paik. Music played a decisive role in his education and training; in 1956, Paik completed a university diploma with a study on Schoenberg. The following year he took summer courses during the Darmstadt Festival, where he discovered the work of K. Stockhausen and, even more importantly, encountered J. Cage. At Parnass Gallery in Wuppertal in 1962, Paik exhibited one of his first works based on an accumulation of television sets, *13 Prepared Televisions*; the title recalls Cage's use of the prepared piano. This "exhibition of electronic music and television" clearly marks one of the very earliest phases of video art. Plugged into 13 tape recorders producing electronic frequencies and thus playing the role of information sources constituting the basis of the signal, the televisions produced all sorts of zigzagging stripes and distortions, visual phenomena resembling "accidents" or "parasites." From the outset, one observes effective interactions of sound and image in this piece. The electronic image is no longer exclusively geared toward the more or less faithful reproduction of reality, just as sound equipment is no longer reserved, in electro-acoustic work, for high-fidelity transmission. The image synthesizer developed by Paik is based on the idea of a mastery of cathodic scanning, after an initial process of decomposition.

In 1970, Paik and the electronic engineer Abe developed one of the first video synthesizers, which Paik called a "light piano." From this point on, the interdependence of sound and the video image comes forth as an essential component of Paik's experimental activity, notably with *Global Groove*. The project includes the presence of John Cage, Charlotte Moorman, and Allen Ginsberg. The sequence centered on Cage constitutes a type of portrait where the composer appears frontally, in close-up; the sound interventions, particularly the confidential tones of Cage's voice, are bathed in silence.

The most significant sequence for Paik's evolution is no doubt the one devoted to Charlotte Moorman, with the appearance of what Paik calls the *TV-Cello*. Three differently sized televisions are linked together vertically by a length of plexiglass. The object is held by the cellist who draws a bow over it; the three screens simultaneously present Moorman playing the *TV-Cello*. Thus the instrument becomes a kind of composite object which allies sound and image in a paradoxical way.

One of the fundamental elements of Paik's work is simultaneity, as well as the unique character of every event capable of producing simultaneity. This is why Paik has explored the possibilities of the satellite on several occasions, conceiving for example an event for thirteen harpsichords broadcast from thirteen different countries, or using live broadcasts transmitted by satellite to organize meetings between Cage and Beuys, Cage and Ginsberg, Cage and McLuhan...

It is of course very difficult to work out a strict classification of categories like performance and multi- (or inter-) media. The very nature of such activities blurs every principle of classification. This is the case, for example, with the actions of Laurie Anderson, who has both a sculptor's and a musician's training. Since the early seventies she has been creating installations, realizing performances, and publishing books. Her first public piece, *Blown Horns* (1972), was qualified as a "concrete concert." In 1974, *As: if* combined text, image, sculpture, and performance, all organized around metaphors. And it was the same year, in *Duet on Ice*, that Anderson used a transformed violin for the first time: the sounds of a violin and those of a recording hidden within the instrument are heard simultaneously. "Since this period," writes A. Labelle-Rojoud, "the musical orientation appears preponderant. However, other aspects of the performance can command one's attention: the length of the work depends on extra-musical givens (the melting time of the ice blocks in which are frozen the blades of the skates she wears), and above all, Laurie Anderson talks, talks, talks between songs, talks about the act of skating, talks about the act of playing the violin, and slides, slides, establishing a parallel between these two activities.[2]"

Germany has provided particularly fertile ground for pluri-artistic creations. Notable among them was Nicolas Schöffer's *Klydex 1*, a "cybernetico-luminodynamic experiment" presented in Hamburg in 1973; Pierre Henry contributed the music and Alvin Nikolaïs the choreography. The spectacle consisted of fifteen sequences, simultaneous or successive, which put metal sculptures equipped with rotating mirrors into movement at varying speeds and incorporated electro-acoustic interventions, vocals, slide and film projections, and dance actions. N. Schöffer had arranged for the public to influence the course of the spectacle by means of five signs that could be used to stop, repeat, accelerate, or slow down the course of events. To this end, five "tallyers" recorded the decisions taken by the public, with the help of a computer to retransmit the majority decision.

The visualization of the musical phenomenon has raised considerable interest lately, to the point where recordings and video clips are more and more frequently produced together. If numerous video pro-

(2) — A. Labelle-Rojoud, *L'acte pour l'art*, Paris, Les Editeurs Evidant, 1988, p. 257.

ductions appear as little more than ersatz items destined to swell sales of recordings by addressing the televisual audience, other creations testify to a desire to "interpret" a piece of music with the means that are specific to the visual universe of cinema and video. Far beyond the simple retransmission of musical phenomena which have been recorded and filmed, *One Plus One* and *Prénom Carmen* by Jean-Luc Godard assuredly represent a full-fledged visual interpretation of music by the Rolling Stones and Beethoven. The same can also be said about recent video creations by Stan Douglas, conceived as veritable instruments of reflection and analysis.

Since the seventies, and at a pace with the increasing complexity of the technologies, multimedia spectacles and environments have not ceased to multiply, most often accumulating poly-sensorial effects and thus becoming the *son et lumière* shows of the international avant-garde. In many cases, the aesthetic aim is confounded with the technical means brought into play, and the interest of the work appears proportional to the scope and seeming innovation of the technical developments.

The list of pluri-artistic installations, often soliciting the spectator's participation, is lengthening at high speed. In this regard it seems necessary to distinguish spectacles where the luminous effects reinforce the overall impact on the public—as in rock concerts—from systems which use technological tools to effect crossovers of contributions from many different media, and from installations conceived in relation to the specific properties of a place and which therefore can simultaneously take on the aspect of a performance.

Reflection and creation on the basis of the environment is also a domain which may concern both musicians and plastic artists, as the projects of Murray Schafer, Pauline Oliveiros, and Luc Ferrari testify.

Nam June Paik

You were very deeply involved with music in the past. Do you think your musical practice has influenced your work up to the present day?

Of course, because from the beginning I started as an electronic composer. Therefore I had all the sounds, anything under ten thousand kilocycles. So I just expanded ten thousand kilocycles to four megacycles, which is the visual range.

So in your case it's technology which is, we could say, the medium that connects you to music.

Yes, because it's always numbers. As musicians, we are accustomed to working with numbers: contrapuntal numbers, harmonic relationships.

So number is the common point for you.

Yes, because we were familiar with numbers. When I started teaching in art school I was surprised because visual artists have no feeling for numbers.

Did your conception of the relationships between sound and image change since your Fluxus production?

Yes, because the TV circuit progressed. The more the technology, the smaller the numbers, or the bigger the numbers; and my concept of art work changes along with them. I don't say I am a "techno-freak" or anything, but everybody has their niche. You know, there are many million people in art, but only the few people who find their niche survive. Whether you can express yourself in that niche or not is not relevant anymore—with the so sad need to put you in a niche. They have the Andy Warhol niche, the Jasper Johns niche... And my niche was that I happened to bump into the area where hardware and software can be better matched. I started, and people want me to do this, so I do. Nowadays of course, since circuit diagrams and microchips progress very quickly, I do that interface.

Do you consider TV as an instrument, like a musical instrument, or as a raw material?

TV I play like piano; and then I made the so-called video synthesizer. Scriabine and Theremin had already done some research in that direction, with some very primitive circuits. So I'm just pursuing that

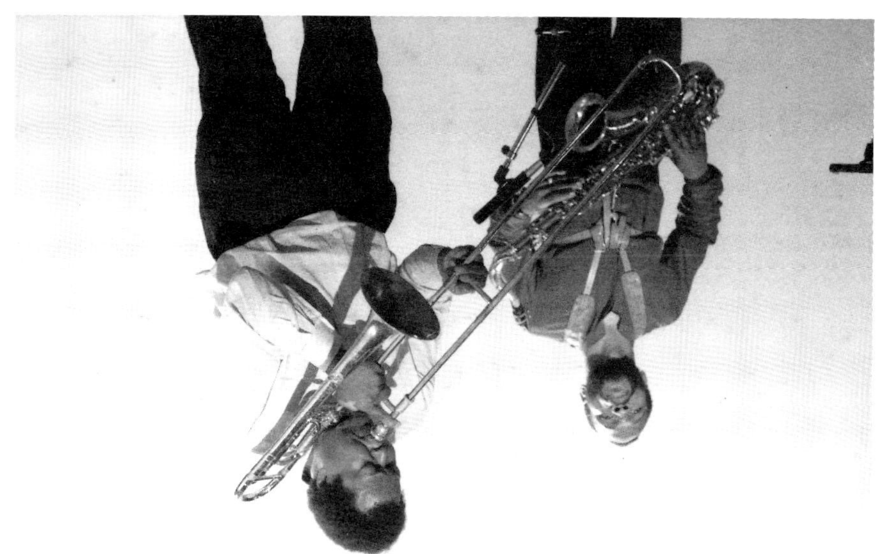

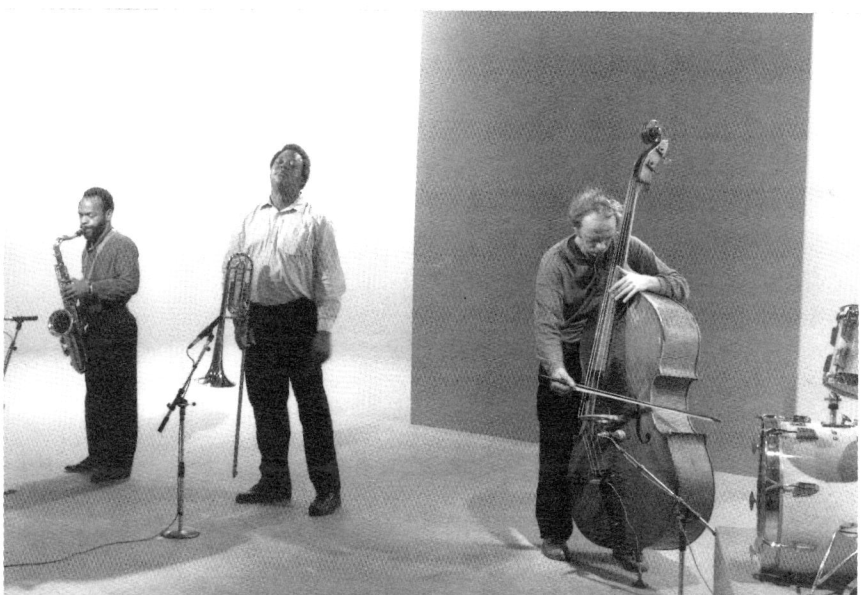

28 - Stan Douglas, *Hors-Champs*, 1992
(© MNAM, Centre Georges Pompidou, Paris)

human dream of a synthesis of sound and vision.

You seem to use TV like prepared piano, because the images are already there and you transform them. Is your work a bit like Cage's use of the prepared piano?

Yes, since I have never been interested in realistic photography, nor in copying something that already exists, because I never had a visual training or talent. I came from sounds, in order to transform a kind of information that I am interested in. You take information, and if it's transformed, you call it lies. And I am more interested in lies than in truth!

Would you consider your work as "intermedia," to borrow the term from Dick Higgins?

Multimedia is in my case closer than intermedia, because I mix different media, whereas intermedia is between two media, I think.

Is the concept of simultaneity important to you?

Yes, centerless information, zero-gravity information, and then "a-causality," asyncronism, all these ideas that you find in Tibetan mandalas. I like that... I tried to make painting in 1959 to make money, and I never could finish, because I always have this fear when I make painting; the next day it doesn't look good enough. You work more, you feel OK, and the next day it's still no good. So I stopped, I quit painting, I never liked painting, but I saw friends doing it and making money... But I failed, and that was my first visual adventure. When I started a new visual adventure using television, I could get away with it, because it orders changes and there's no center.

More precisely, are the flexible or fugitive aspects of your video installations very important to you?

Flexibility is a necessary part, because unlike painting, video art can be very bad because of technical constraints. A very fat margin of error subsists. Painting, once you've painted, is fairly stable, but we often have to do it all over again.

Does this taste for change come from your past as a musician?

It's very important, because I think that the perfection, the harmony which exists in painting, exists in performance art as ecstasy. Ecstasy is going out of yourself, it is a very temporal, time-based concept. So if you get great ecstasy one day, one night, you know, it just ends after the concert. So for me, the harmony or perfection was always temporal. That's why we need a moving picture, because we don't believe in the eternal truth.

Do you still think that musical avant-garde is dominated by purity of means and the questioning of conceptual systems?

That's a very good question, because one of the hardest things in the world is to make a good avant-garde classical music. You know, like John Cage. I mean, music that gets you thinking, with complex, challenging sounds. You can easily find a hundred great visual artists in the world after World War II, ten pop artists, ten new realists, ten video artists maybe—but great composers in the classic sense, less than ten, or even less than five. After Phil Glass, maybe nobody; and Phil Glass is already a product of 1972. After 1972, we have fifty great visual artists, but no composers. It's a very hard discipline.

I made two great musical discoveries in my life, and I'm trying to make them performable by other artists. I'm making a video opera, which was a big success in New York and will be presented next October at the Festival of Donaueschingen. By comparison to the so-called "grand opera" of Verdi or Wagner, where the music stays the same and everything else is different, in my video opera the pictures stay the same, but we change everything else. Because I made a lot of video pieces with John Cage, Merce Cunnigham, Allen Ginsberg, and so on, for twenty years, and all these are very important, classic. All right, but when we play it, it's boring. So I took a Merce Cunningham piece and I stripped down everything, and when we project it, we simply do rock'n'roll with it. And it was a big success! I also worked with a punk-rock group from New York, called the Bad Brains. We played that with a Joseph Beuys video, and it was perfect harmony. And next we played a Merce Cunningham video tape with a live performance by Simon Walted. It was an absolute success.

I have another piece which involves banging a piano with a camera: visual and sound, it's very effective. And then I did other improvisations, but since I'm sixty I may die in five years... so I decided to write all that down. I also decided to make a few compositions. Last night in Paris I made some great songs. It's nearly as good as Phil Glass, but different, very different.

I have a string quartet that I wrote in 1956, and a chamber orchestra for nine instruments that I wrote in 1957; it's never been played, but I'll test it, and then I'll write some more new themes. I tell you, I am determined to stay in music! Because I am in the most venerated, the most important music dictionary, yes, the *Riman*. And I got half a page...

Is collage a notion that fits into your current preoccupations?

Yes, I think so. The small anecdote is that I wanted to come and live in France in 1958; at that point I was living in Freiburg, Germany, and I was doing music studies with Wolfgang Fortner. That was when I started to get interested in collage—still in the musical domain. During the summer I had written a piece of chamber music, and Fortner, who liked it a lot, and even recommended it to Bruno Madelna for a performance. So I wrote a letter to Pierre Schaeffer, but he never answered. I met him later and said "Look Pierre, you didn't answer my letter." And he said, "Oh I'm sorry," he said he regretted it. So he remembered. I did everything to get into his seminar, but he didn't answer, so I went to Cologne.

When you work on TV installations, do you intend to compose new sets of images or to decompose existing ones?

All that was a game, composition and decomposition, it was all invented by semiotics people and fashionable postmodernists. But decomposition or composition is the same thing.

Do you feel that the perception of sound and the perception of images are two radically different phenomena?

Of course. Because I think sound goes very deep, is very emotional, and has a very exclusive quality. When you have one sound, you cannot listen to another sound, when somebody plays the radio, you cannot do anything about it. Whereas the visual is more freedom oriented, more reason oriented. So you can have a hundred paintings but you can only have one music. Music is definitely more dictator oriented, so that's why all dictators use music and not that much museum/video stuff. When music is good, it is very strong, much stronger than visual experience. Sound alone is much more strong and profound than sound and picture together. For instance, if you ask me to write a musical composition of seven minutes, it may take one year to be good, but you ask me to make seven minutes with a video tape, I can make it like that. So sound alone is very hard, and I have great respect for composers.

Do you think that your artistic attitude runs parallel to the development and amplification of technological means, or do you consider that it represents a criticism of technological power?

I think people like to hear me say I am more critical of technology than for technology, and I suppose my taste is not exactly pro-technological. I am very clumsy, and I don't dress like a computer program. You understand, I am very clumsy at pushing buttons, I cannot even play a CD, I can barely play LPs and turn on the radio, I have a hard time operating the audio cassette. Therefore, technology and me is like a mariage at gunpoint. So my attitude to technology is very dadaistic. I'm not for "smooth" technological things. But now everybody is *for* or *against* technology. It's a cliché in both cases. I play a kind of game in between, sometimes here, sometimes there.

There's a kind of tension between the two.

Yes, I'm not like the normal ecology people, you know, because they are unrealistic too.

Do you feel a certain community with the younger generations of artists who create video installations?

I am number one, but I'm happy if more people work in video:

that makes me more important. But I hope that people don't say they are just copying me. Video gives such a wide range of choice and now many young guys are working very independently; they have nothing to do with me except that they use TV, and everybody is using TV. Anyway, TV is not my invention, so they can use TV too.

Do you get your ideas through contact with technological means, or do you already have something in mind before starting to work?

I wrote in a 1963 article that I have absolutely no preconception of the art work. I just see what is available as a means, then I look for the unusual connections of two or three means. So technology determines my work in art. And especially the technology of yesterday, after it becomes cheap. As soon as technology becomes junk, then we have access to it also. Video equipment, computers, and so on, change very quickly. And when they change, I make a concept to use them as new sources. So we constantly make tools, and the tools define us.

Is it the same with sounds, do the ideas come through the means you have?

I worked a lot with the cellist Charlotte Moorman; I've also used prepared piano quite a lot. I sometimes use soprano singers too... I wrote five or six songs in Korea in 1947. I've been thinking how to improve them since 1947, and now I think I have answer.

You seem to enjoy going from one style of music to another, and mixing them. Is it important for you to carry out a kind of collage of different artists, as in your video opera?

Yes, it's also because I don't have enough time to do it all myself. Number one I am old, and number two I haven't got much time, so I have to build up people to perform what I propose. I also must publish and record—most importantly publish, so my music can be played after my death, like Beethoven!

(Paris, June 6, 1992)

Stan Douglas

In Paris I became aware of the whole phenomenon of free jazz, which was called the "new thing" in the U.S. and "free jazz" in France. It was an idiom of black American music which had done away with certain conventions of rhythm or harmonic coherence, where certain liberties could be taken. It wasn't so simple, because even when the music seemed offhand it was always highly structured: it wasn't just play the head song, first chorus, another chorus, solo, solo, solo, then head again, then the end. There was more liberty taken in what the musicians could play. In America, this was related to some of the musicians' affiliations with black nationalism, but in France it also had other connotations; it was particularly popular around the time of May 68. At that time, audiences for free-jazz concerts could number in the thousands, and the socialist and communist parties even organized concerts of free jazz, because they regarded it as an ideal of social organization.

In *Hors-Champs*[1], we used video to show how we saw a piece of free jazz, in the manner of the ORTF televised music productions of the 60s. You see the same kind of placelessness, the use of a studio as a sort of laboratory, a nowhere kind of place defined by false walls and a curious kind of light, all filmed in black and white. In those productions, though, they would typically shoot a piece with 45 cameras, but we used only two. In the installation there is a large suspended wall: on one side you see the official version of the program, and on the back side you see the unofficial program. When camera A is on the front side, camera B is on the back, and vice-versa; so it's like an automatic counterpart to the official version of the program. On the back side we also see the drummer and the bass player, because the solo is not as highlighted as it would be on the front. We also get to see that the camera is unsteady, it's framing, setting up for a shot, etc., all things which were typically left out. One of the primary features of the project is the Albert Ayler piece we take as its basis, which is called *Spirits Rejoice*, from 1966. It uses four

(1) — *Hors-Champs*, video-sound installation produced by the MNAM, Georges Pompidou Center, within the famework of a one-person exhibition presented at the Center in December 1993.

main musical motives: call and response, gospel song, military fanfare, and also the Marseillaise, and this calls up all the history that I'm trying to remember in the piece.

When you work with music, is your intention to show how theatrical it is?

It is a time-based medium, it's often a performative medium, but I'm more interested in music as it resembles my other kinds of work; music as a cultural precipitate, or something that represents its social situation. It's interesting the way in which music contains the meaning of the culture which produced it.

And you think that video is the right media to show what music contains?

Not necessarily; music is music. And there is always a compromise if you try to frame that music through another form, through a written form or a visual form. This piece *Hors Champs* very self-consciously indicates the limits of what can be represented; in a way, it's saying that there's always an elsewhere of meaning, of representation, always something that's not there. We have two cameras, and we have been able to resurrect the material that would normally be thrown away in production offices, but there are still other points of view, other considerations of the music. One thing peculiar to that shooting style was that there's always the sense of a control coming from somewhere; there is some exterior plan which frames the music, and this is very self-consciously made evident throughout the piece.

Do you consider yourself as an interpreter who adds a kind of counterpoint to what musicians do?

I've tried to form some sort of dialogue with the musical work: not necessarily to represent it, not to interpret it in any kind of conclusive way, but to present another response to the music. It is music, music was created for the project; but the project represents music in a certain limited way. A piece of music is always changing, there are many aspects of the piece which we didn't see; the music was constantly developing through every attempt to get a good version, it is never complete.

Did you decide with the musicians on the duration of the piece?

Yes, we listened to it, we saw how things were going, and added to the piece as we went along. The kinds of shots we were doing were based quite explicitly on the score: there are certain sections, certain musical changes, and basically one camera would be on a certain scene during that segment of the music. The other camera was free to attend to whatever was going on in the space, to see how the musicians reacted to the focus of attention, but then that camera had to be listening carefully to the music so as to be in place when the segment that it was supposed to present came up. So the cameramen and myself had to listen very carefully to be in the right place as the music was going on, to listen and collaborate with the music.

The cameras are like silent instruments?

Yes, exactly.

When you do a video installation, how does the idea come, for instance the idea of the screen with both sides: does it come after, or do you have a process at the origin?

Everything develops more or less organically, I mean, the idea crystallizes little by little. I was invited to do a project in France, and I wanted to do something peculiar to France that would somehow implicate my coming to France; this history of immigration which is now more or less over had always seemed interesting to me. But then there is a whole series of dualities in the piece, America and Europe, French and English, black and white, and the opposition of the two parts of the screen.

And you consider the result as a sort of entity between sound and image?

Everything performs in concert, all aspects are interrelated. It's like a transparency, a screen through which we can see the music; the music is affected by the way in which it's seen, and what is seen is affected by the music. The way one understands the music is based on what we see on the screen, and how we inhabit the space.

(Paris, May 29, 1992)

JOHN CAGE (1912-1992, Los Angeles)

Although a student of Schoenberg, Cage was never a convert to the dodecaphonic system. Considered the inventor of the happening (*Black Mountain*, 1952), he allowed the effects of chance to reach all the way to the score itself. Cage's thought and music have constituted an essential influence for several generations of artists. Far from being limited to the world of music, his creations pose much larger questions as to the status of the art work in society, and the relations of art to life and to the environment. His field of activity englobed the most diverse concerns, from the musical score to performances, books, graphic works.

STAN DOUGLAS

Born in 1960 in Vancouver, Canada, he attended the Emily Carr College of Arts (interdisciplinary studies). Among his principle works are: *Overture* 1986 (cinematographic installation); *Samuel Beckett: Teleplays*, 1988 (traveling exhibition and catalogue around Beckett's telvisual work); *Monodramas*, 1991 (10 televised spots); *Hors-Champs*, 1992. In addition to his own artistic activity, he has contributed to numerous critical works on art and cultural politics (notably *Vancouver Anthology: the Institutional Politics of Art*). He is now preparing an exhibition at the Georges Pompidou Center (December 1993).

MILAN GRYGAR

Born in 1926 in Czechoslovakia, M. Grygar, plastic artist and musician, lives and works in Prague. Since 1965, his work has been based on the organic relation between plastic images and sound, and on the plastic time which it produces. He is represented, among others, in the collections at the Stedelijk Museum in Amsterdam, the National Museum of Osaka, and the Georges Pompidou Center in Paris.

MILAN KNIZAK

Born in Prague in 1940, he began working with the plastic arts in the sixties, creating what he calls "broken music" with records manipulated both visually and acoustically. Founder of the group "Aktual" in Prague, he also kept up close contacts with the Fluxus movement. One of his recent installations was presented at the Musée d'Art Moderne de la Ville de Paris during an exhibition on Czech artists.

FRANCIS MIROGLIO

Born in Marseille in 1924, Francis Miroglio studied with Darius Milhaud at the Paris Conservatoire. As the founder, in 1965, of the Nuits de la Fondation Maeght, a festival for contemporary music, painting and sculpture, he is active in several domains, as a poet, librettist, composer, plastic artist and sculptor, and seeks in particular to bring to the fore a dialectic of visual and sonorous density in his work. F. Miroglio, an outstanding personality for musical creation over the last decades, is carrying out several programs of research in the fields of open forms and aleatory music.

NAM JUNE PAIK

Born in 1932 in Seoul, Korea, he left his country in 1949 for Hong Kong and Tokyo, where he studied aesthetics, art history, and music. In 1956-57 the young composer/performer moved to Germany, where he met first K. Stockhausen, who introduced him to electronic music, then J. Cage. In the course of the sixties he participated in the activities of Fluxus. Paik began to create audio-visual pieces or video sculptures in 1964 in the United States, pioneering the use of television as a tool — and no longer just a transmission medium — for experiments with new forms of language, based on spectacular TV-set installations.

TOM PHILLIPS

Tom Phillips was born in London in 1937. His oeuvre, characterized by its extreme diversity, includes books (*A Humument, Dante's Hell,* translated and illustrated by the author), films (*A TV Dante,* with Peter Greenaway), scores and records... The wide variety of supports employed by T. Phillips nevertheless remains closely dependent on the nature of the artistic project he is working on at any one time.

TAKIS

Born in 1925 in Athens, Takis moved to Paris in 1954. Drawing inspiration from the modern world, he integrates motors and magnetic forces into his works, which become an integral, active part of his sculptures. Takis is accepted as being one of the founder figures in the sound sculpture movement. He has taken part in several exhibitions and musical events throughout the world.

WOLF VOSTELL

Born in 1930 in Leverkusen, W. Vostell was, along with Beuys, one of the key figures of the Fluxus movement in Germany. He is the mainspring of "dé-coll/age" (posters, letters, torn photographs) which he applied with extremely dissimilar techniques, such as installations, actions, video art, multi-media. Several exhibitions were devoted to his work in 1992 (in Bonn, Leverkusen, Mannheim, Mühlheim/Ruhr).

IANNIS XENAKIS

Born in 1922, I. Xenakis was a student at the Polytechnic Institute in Athens. He worked on musical composition under Hermann Scherchen, then Olivier Messiaen at the Paris Conservatoire. He collaborated with Le Corbusier as an engineer and architect between 1947 and 1960. I. Xenakis was the founder of the concept of musical masses, of "stochastic" music which gave rise to the calculation of probabilities and set theory. In 1967, he created, among others, the first *Polytope* for the French Pavilion of the Universal Exhibition in Montreal. Subsequent works testify to his interest in the link between visual and sound mediums, in particular "Persepolis" (1971), the Polytopes of Cluny (1972) and of Mycenae (1978) and the Diatope for the inauguration of the Pompidou Center (1978).

Armengaud, Jean-Pierre, *La musique chauve de Jean Dubuffet*, Ed.Séguier, Paris, 1991
Beuys, Joseph, *Bâtissons une cathédrale*, Ed.de l'Arche, Paris, 1988
Block, Ursula et Glasmeier Michael, *Broken Music*, Daadgalerie Berlin, Gemeentemuseum Den Haag, Magasin Grenoble, 1989
Bosseur, Dominique et Jean-Yves, *Révolutions musicales*, Ed.Minerve, Paris, 1986
Bosseur, Jean-Yves, *Musique, passion d'artistes*, Ed.Skira, Lausanne, 1991
Bosseur, Jean-Yves, *Vocabulaire de la musique contemporaine*, Ed.Minerve, Paris, 1992
Calas, Héléna et Nicolas, *Takis*, Galilée, Paris, 1984
Cage, John, *Silence*, Wesleyan University Press, Middletown, 1961
Cage, John, *A Year from monday*, Wesleyan University Press, Middletown, 1963
Cage, John, *Notation*, Something else Press, New-York, 1969
Cage, John, To *describe the process of composition used in Not wanting to say anything about Marcel*, EYE Editions, Cincinnati, 1969
Cage, John, *M. Writings '67-'72*, Calder and Boyars, 1973
Cage, John, *Pour les oiseaux* (entretiens avec Daniel Charles), Ed.Belfond, Paris, 1976
Cage, John, *Empty words*, Wesleyan University Press, Middletown, 1979
Cage, John, *X*, Wesleyan University Press, Middletown, 1986
Cage, John, *Le livre des champignons* (trad. Pierre Lartigue), Ed. Ryôan-Ji, Marseille, 1983
Cage, John, *Mirage verbal, Writings through Marcel Duchamp, notes,* (introduction de Pierre Lartigue), Ed. Ulysse Fin de Siècle, Dijon, 1990
Charles, Daniel, *Gloses sur J. Cage*, Ed. Christian.Bourgois 10/18, Paris 1978
Eco, Umberto, *L'oeuvre ouverte*, Ed. du Seuil, Paris, 1965
Chopin, Henri, *Poésie sonore internationale*, Ed.Jean-Michel Place, Paris, 1979
Heidsieck, Bernard, *Partition V*, Ed.du Soleil Noir, Paris, 1973
Kagel, Mauricio, *Tam-tam*, Ed.Christian Bourgois, Paris, 1983
Karkoschka, Erhard, *Das Schriftbild der Neuen Musik*, Moeck, Celle, 1966
Kostelanetz, Richard, *The Theatre of Mixed Means*, the Dial Press, New-York, 1968
Kostelanetz, Richard, *Conversing with J. Cage*, Limelight Editions, New-York, 1988
Kostelanetz, Richard, *John Cage, an Anthology*, Da Capo Press, New-York, 1991
Labelle-Rojoux, Arnaud, *L'acte pour l'art*, Les Editeurs Evidant, Paris, 1988
La Monte Young et Jackson Mac Low, *An Anthology*, Heiner Friedrich, Münich, 1970
La Monte Young et Marian Zazeela, *Selected Writings*, George Wittenborn, New-York, 1970
Lambert, Jean-Clarence, *Dépassement de l'art ?* Ed. Anthropos, Paris 1974
De La Motte-Haber, Helga, *Musik und bildende Kunst*, Laaber verlag, Laaber, 1990
von Maur, Karin, *Vom Klang der Bilder*, Ed.Prestel, Münich, 1983
Nyman, Michael, *Experimental Music*, Studio Vista, Londres, 1974
Phillips, Tom, *Works, Texts (to 1974)*, Hansjörg Mayer, Stuttgart, 1975
Ori, Luciano, *Musica Visiva*, La casa Usher, Florence, 1987
Popper, Franck, *Art, action et participation*, Ed.Klincksieck, Paris, 1980
Revault d'Allonnes, Olivier, *Les Polytopes de Iannis Xenakis*, Ed.Balland, Paris, 1975
Schnebel, Dieter, Mauricio Kagel, *Musik, Theater, Film*, Du Mont Schauberg, Cologne, 1970
Schnebel, Dieter, *Mo-No, Musik zum Lesen*, Du Mont Schauberg, Cologne, 1069
Schnebel, Dieter, *Denkbare Musik*, Du Mont Schauberg, Cologne, 1972
Vostell, Wolf, *Happening & Leben*, Hermann Luchterhand Verlag, Berlin, 1970
Wedewer, Rolf, *Wolf Vostell*, Ed.Braus, 1992
Xenakis, Iannis, *Musique, Architecture*, Casterman-poche, Paris, 1976
Xenakis, Iannis, *Arts/Sciences/Alliages*, Casterman, Paris, 1979

catalogues, revues...

A Noise in your Eye, an International Exhibition of Sound Sculpture, Arnolfini, Bristol, 1985
Ecouter par les yeux, objets et environnements sonores, Arc, Musée d'Art Moderne de la Ville de Paris, 1980
John Cage, Revue d'Esthétique, n° 13-14-15, Ed.Privat, Toulouse, 1988 *François Dufrêne*, Musée d'Art Moderne de Villeneuve d'Ascq, 1988
Milan Grygar, Maison du livre, de l'image et du son, Villeurbanne, 1992
Francis Miroglio, les Cahiers du CREM (Centre de Recherches en Esthétique Musicale), n°6-7, Mont Saint-Aignan, 1988
La musique lettriste, La revue Musicale, n°282-283, Ed.Richard-Masse, Paris 1971
Max Neuhaus, Edition du Centre d'Art, Domaine de Kerguehennec, 1987
L'oeil musicien, Palais des Beaux-Arts, Charleroi, Ed.Lebeer-Hossmann, Bruxelles, 1985
Nam June Paik, Whitney Museum, New York, 1982
Sarkis, Le Magasin (Centre d'art contemporain de Grenoble), 1992
Jean Tinguely, Centre Georges Pompidou, dir. Pontus-Hulten, Paris, 1988

CONTENTS

Achevé d'imprimer
par Mame Imprimeurs à Tours
Dépôt légal : Février 1993
N° 29619